"If you're tired of waiting on your childr[...] a
Happy Mom will liberate you!" —**Dr. K**[...] g
author of *Have a New Kid by Friday* an[...]

"*31 Days to Becoming a Happy Mom* is a practical, easy-to-read guide to growth toward happiness. You owe it to yourself, and your children deserve it. I highly recommend this book." —**Gary Chapman,** PhD, author of *The Five Love Languages*

"Moms, get ready to take a much needed break. Pick up this book to find refreshment and nourishment for your mommy soul!" —**Jill Savage,** CEO of Hearts at Home and author of *No More Perfect Moms*

"This is a big-idea book—wrapped in plain language and real-life stories. This book continues the tradition of offering positive, powerful help—right where all of us need it!" —**Dr. David and Lisa Frisbie,** executive directors, Healthy Habits for Parents and Families

"*31 Days to Becoming a Happy Mom* is more than helpful. It is life-changing! Arlene knows how to be a godly, great mom and she shows you how to be one too. After reading this book, you and your kids will be a lot happier and a lot healthier!" —**Dr. David Clarke,** psychologist, speaker, and author of *I Don't Want a Divorce* and *Married But Lonely*

"Arlene is a bright light and in this book she will be your daily dose of encouragement as you seek to become part of the minority elite who've figured out how to mother the happy way." —**Dannah Gresh,** creator, Secret Keeper Girl®

"If you're ready to take mothering to the next level and joyfully accept God's calling for you, then read *31 Days to Becoming a Happy Mom*. Arlene candidly gives you the tools you'll need to be the parent you want to be." —**Dave Stone,** senior pastor of Southeast Christian Church, Louisville, KY, and author of the Faithful Families series

"Happy, healthy, and heart-for-God kids are a reflection of a happy, healthy, and heart-for-God mom. Arlene loves being a mother and she loves equipping, encouraging, and empowering moms to love God and love their high-calling. *31 Days to Becoming a Happy Mom* is a must-read." —**Pam Farrel,** author of 40 books, including *Men Are Like Waffles, Women Are Like Spaghetti*

"Arlene Pellicane brings us welcome words of wisdom to becoming the happy mom we've always dreamed of being. Filled with practical insights and biblical truth, this book leads every mom to having a happy home." —**Karol Ladd,** author of *The Power of a Positive Mom*

"If you're feeling overwhelmed, underappreciated, and exhausted more often than not, this book will help you rediscover the joys of motherhood while helping you get a game plan for success, no matter what your kids' ages." —**Amy Groeschel,** women's pastor of LifeChurch.tv, coauthor of *From This Day Forward: Five Commitments to Fail-Proof Your Marriage*

"*31 Days to Becoming a Happy Mom*—could a title be more spot-on and reassuring? As a woman who considers being a mom the most influential, demanding, joy-filled job I ever undertook, I wholeheartedly recommend this book." —**Kendra Smiley,** speaker and author of several books, including *Journey of a Strong-Willed Child*

"Forget being perfect. Throw out the mommy guilt. Arlene opens our eyes to biblical, practical ways to put the fun back in motherhood in doable, bite-size nuggets. A must-read for all moms." —**Sharon Jaynes,** author of 18 books, including *Praying for Your Husband from Head to Toe*

"If you've ever felt overwhelmed with the pressures of being a mom, this book is for you. Arlene's practical game plan for mothering will change your life and the lives of those you love." —**Gwen Smith,** speaker, worship leader, and author of *Broken into Beautiful*

"Arlene Pellicane's words will lift you up, point you to Jesus, and help you confidently carry out the all-important, sometimes crazy, but completely holy calling of raising your kids for God's glory. The ultimate mom manual!" —**Karen Ehman,** New York Times bestselling author of *Keep It Shut: What to Say, How to Say It, and When to Say Nothing at All*

"Arlene has done a masterful job providing tools that will transform you, your children, and your marriage into a home of joy. *31 Days to Becoming a Happy Mom* is humorous, inspiring, practical, helpful, and hopeful." —**Fern Nichols,** founder, Moms in Prayer International

Becoming

a Happy

Mom

Arlene Pellicane

HARVEST HOUSE PUBLISHERS
EUGENE, OREGON

Cover by Left Coast Design, Portland, Oregon

Cover photo © Warren Goldswain / Shutterstock

31 DAYS TO BECOMING A HAPPY MOM
Copyright © 2015 by Arlene Pellicane
Published by Harvest House Publishers
Eugene, Oregon 97402
www.harvesthousepublishers.com

Library of Congress Cataloging-in-Publication Data
   Pellicane, Arlene, 1971-
     31 days to becoming a happy mom / Arlene Pellicane.
       pages cm
     Includes bibliographical references.
     ISBN 978-0-7369-6350-3 (pbk.)
     ISBN 978-0-7369-6351-0 (eBook)
     1. Motherhood--Religious aspects--Christianity. 2. Mothers--Prayers and devotions. I. Title. II. Title: Thirty-one days to becoming a happy mom.
     BV4529.18.P45 2015
     248.8'431--dc23

                             2015008347

Printed in the United States of America

15 16 17 18 19 20 21 22 23 / BP-KBD / 10 9 8 7 6 5 4 3 2 1

To my mom
I don't know anyone who is a happier mom than you.
Thank you for putting the happy in my childhood and bringing
me joy each day.

Contents

Introduction

Ditch the Crowd

When my son Ethan was in first grade, we had this little talk after he received an academic award.

"I'm so proud that you are well behaved at school," I said beaming.

"Oh yes," Ethan replied. "I'm very well behaved at school. I'm much worse at home because I fight with Noelle!"

Isn't it true we can be well behaved and pleasant with others, but we have a much harder time acting happy and agreeable with family members? As a mom, you've picked up this book because you know how it feels to start the day like Mary Poppins and go to bed as Cruella De Vil. Why are moms today stressed out, pooped out, and overwhelmed much of the time? Part of the answer lies in this quote from Erma Bombeck:

> Do you know what you call those who use towels and never wash them, eat meals and never do the dishes, sit in rooms they never clean, and are entertained till they drop? If you have just answered, "A house guest," you're wrong because I have just described my kids.[1]

If that scenario sounds familiar, get ready for a change! You are not running a hotel; you are managing a home. You don't have guests to cater to; you have children to raise. We can easily get caught up in the mommy culture around us where the roles have been hijacked. Kids are calling the shots and moms are taking the orders. When that happens, unhappiness reigns supreme, not just for moms, but for kids too.

According to a Barna study, 8 in 10 moms feel overwhelmed by stress and 7 out of 10 say they do not get enough rest. Only 19 percent of moms report being extremely satisfied as a mom.[2] It's my goal to move you into this 19 percent by the time you're done reading this book.

It's time to ditch the mommy crowd, epitomized by a woman I met at a thrift store. (This isn't a slam against thrift stores; I was there too!) This mom had three children clinging to her as she tried to move up and down the aisles (operative word: *tried*). They cried, whined, and bellyached for all to hear. Then one of them punched me in the leg. The mom apologized profusely. As I stood in the checkout line, I watched this mom dragging her five-year-old like a rag doll under her arm as that child cried so hysterically it sounded like cackling. Who in that situation could be a happy mom?

It's time for a revival of good old common sense in motherhood today. We can mine wisdom from trusted guides. That's why I've asked my author friends to chime in. My children Ethan, Noelle, and Lucy are ten, eight, and five, so I interviewed moms who are farther down the road than I am. You'll hear from proud grandmas, mothers of teens, and even a State Mother of the Year. You'll read insights from single moms and stepmoms. As you read with an open heart in the safe environment of these pages, you'll not only find friends and cheerleaders along the way. You'll find mentors worthy of learning from.

Circle the Important Stuff

I thought my husband, James, was crazy. He wanted our fifth grader and our third grader to read a business book with us, *The Compound Effect* by Darren Hardy.[3] This seemed a little advanced for our elementary school entrepreneurs of tomorrow.

Despite my doubts, Ethan took off, reading easily and grasping the material. Noelle, our third grader, needed more help. After all, chapter 1 had words like *sensibilities, commercialism,* and *deprivation.* Compound interest isn't exactly on a third grader's radar screen. We knew she couldn't read the book on her own. It would be too overwhelming and she would quit. So she and I sat side by side. She would read a few paragraphs and then I would read a few paragraphs. When we got to a word she didn't recognize, she circled it. I explained what the word meant until she understood. She focused her attention on the words she circled. Not only was she getting a vocabulary lesson, she was spending quality time with Mom and learning valuable life lessons at the same time.

Like Noelle reading her book with pen in hand, I want you to picture motherhood as a book that can be marked up. Put a big circle around the important stuff. Mistakes can be crossed out in red with "Note to self: Don't do this again" scrawled in the margin. Yet we tend to emphasize the words and activities that are secondary: make cupcakes, drive to soccer, buy costumes, browse Pinterest for decorating ideas. There's nothing wrong with any of these pursuits unless, of course, there is nothing else circled in our mom life. Mother of five, Rhonda Rhea, says it this way,

> If there's fuzz all over the family room carpet, ten years down the road no one is going to care. If the girls go to church with really bad hair, and even if everyone there thinks you're a terrible mother because of it, that doesn't really matter. Don't focus on being the perfect mother, focus on raising godly children. Instead of thinking *What does my home look like?* or *What do I look like?* think *What is in the hearts of my kids?*[4]

Known as the positive mom, author Karol Ladd agrees that circling the small stuff can skew our perspective. Getting to the movies late one day, her family had no other choice than to sit in the front row of the theater. The battle scenes were too close, the images too intense, and the whole experience was painful. They went to see the movie again another day and sat in the middle of the theater so they could get the full perspective of the movie as it was meant to be seen. Karol says,

> In the same way, the happy mom has to step back, not only to be flexible but also to think of the big picture. In ten years, will this really matter? What can I teach my child from this? In view of eternity, will this make any difference? Often what is happening in the moment seems so big, whether it's something at school or something that our kids did, and it seems so much larger than life. But if we as moms can step back and think of what God wants to teach us through it, it looks different. I wish someone would have told me to keep the bigger picture in mind.[5]

The Five Keys to Happiness for Moms

For the next thirty-one days, you're going to draw a big circle around becoming a happier mom. Why is this important anyway? Maybe to you it sounds downright selfish. Well, consider the alternative. If you are an unhappy mom, griping about life, snapping at your kids, breathing empty threats, and living in perpetual gray, how does that serve your family? How does that make your relationship with God attractive? Believe me, living with joy is hardly selfish. Being a happy mom may be the greatest way to serve your kids at this age and stage.

But maybe you don't *feel* like smiling. Don't worry. As you focus on these five keys to happiness, using the acronym HAPPY, I promise you will find it easier to smile again and often. You are going to become more...

H = Healthy
A = Action-Oriented
P = Prayerful
P = Perseverant
Y = Yes-Filled

Being *healthy* isn't just for gym rats and nutritionists. The mom who cares for others must first tend to herself by exercising, eating well, and resting. You need spiritual and emotional reserves to lead your children well. You can't impart overall health to your kids if you don't possess it yourself.

When a mom is *action-oriented*, she doesn't discipline with a harsh tone, yelling, or empty threats. She doesn't get ugly; she doesn't give long lectures. She acts as a leader. She makes changes when necessary and enforces consequences with consistency. You're going to learn how to eliminate the mom mantra, "How many times do I have to tell you to...?"

You should be more *prayerful*, but how do you find the time? Does prayer really make a difference? Is there something else to pray besides "Help!" and "Bless my children"? You'll learn that becoming a praying mama gives you an edge like nothing else.

Persevering is tough. Motherhood isn't a sprint; it's a marathon. Too many moms give up too easily when something doesn't work the first couple of times. Tenacity, grit, resolve—these are the characteristics the modern mom desperately needs. You are in it to win it.

Being *yes-filled* means you look at motherhood as a huge positive in your life, not a negative. Instead of feeling like "my life is over now that I'm a mom," you see the future and it's bright. There's nothing wrong at times with saying no (you and your kids need that), but this key will help you embrace the yeses in motherhood.

How to Get the Most Out of This Book

I've noticed two kinds of people in life. There are "Tell me more" people and "I already know that" people. The "Tell me more" person picks up a book like my *31 Days to a Happy Husband* and says, "I've been happily married for forty years, but I'm sure there's something else I could learn." The "I already know that" person picks up the same book and says, "If I don't have it figured out by now, it's never gonna happen."

My middle child, Noelle, has often said "I already know that" in response to her older brother's unsolicited advice. That's funny when you're eight, defending yourself against your know-it-all sibling. But for us moms, the "I already know that" attitude is toxic. It shores up our defenses and keeps our hearts closed off from true transformation.

As you encounter concepts in this book, I urge you not to default to "I already know that." Instead, think "Tell me more." You'll see old ideas with new eyes. This way of reading makes all the difference between a changed life and a life that remains static and stale.

You can read one chapter each day for thirty-one consecutive days, or you may read several chapters in one sitting. Or read just one chapter each week (guilt-free because you are a busy mom). Tailor your reading experience to what will work for your mom life. To keep on track, you can:

Start a Happy Moms Discussion Group. You can read the book together with a group of moms, or even just one other mom who also wants to become a happier mom. Use the discussion guide on pages 200-205. It's ideal to meet weekly for six weeks to talk about what you're learning and to set up a doable start and stop date.

Take the boost. At the end of each day's reading, you'll find an action step and prayer: your daily energy boost. It won't take much time, but if you take the boosts consistently, your family will see a difference. Keep in mind your children can't see the good intentions in your heart. What they notice is your behavior, what you say and do, for better or worse. This month, make it for the better.

Think on God's Word. You'll find a list of Bible verses to encourage you to become a more joy-filled mom on pages 197-199. You can read these aloud or think about them throughout your day. Put verses on your bathroom mirror, over the kitchen sink, anywhere to remind you of God's goodness and the high calling you enjoy as a mother.

Remember the business book Noelle and I were reading, *The Compound Effect?* It's so fitting for us here because that book is all about doing small, seemingly inconsequential things over time. The payoff takes a while to see, but when it comes, it's huge. That's the same potential you have right now as a mother. You will be making small, positive changes that may seem very insignificant at the time. But as the years roll by, the minor adjustments you make now may be the difference between a close relationship with your children or a distant one.

A few nights ago, I went to the bathroom in the middle of the night. Then I shuffled to the girls' room to check if they had their blankets on. Lucy had her neck bent so dramatically that her body looked like a candy cane. I thought if I slept like that, I'd have a crick in my neck for days. I straightened her body out. Her blanket was crumpled at the foot of the bed, so I spread it over her body on that cold night. I tried to move quietly, but she woke up.

"I'm just putting the blanket on you," I whispered.

"Goodnight, Mom," she said, unaware of the chiropractic treatment that had been averted.

As I walked back into my room, a sense of joy filled my heart. *I get to be that little angelic creature's mom* (remember, she was sleeping). *I'm needed. I am blessed.* Some days, that appreciation for being a mom overwhelms us like the tide. But most days, we don't see the joy in putting blankets over little candy canes. We interpret it as work—lots of endless work.

It's time to put a little more fun into our work. With the guidance of the Holy Spirit, you're going to be transported to a much happier, more appreciative place as a mother.

Get ready. Help is on the way!

Are You a Happy Mom?

Before you begin reading Day 1, take this self-assessment to gauge how happy you are as a mom right now. There are no correct answers, no other moms peering over your shoulder to compare themselves against you. Read each statement and circle if you mostly agree or disagree.

1. I am not overwhelmed or stressed by motherhood on most days.

    ❏ Agree   ❏ Disagree

2. My children are respectful and well behaved.

    ❏ Agree   ❏ Disagree

3. I don't yell at my kids.

    ❏ Agree   ❏ Disagree

4. My kids do what I tell them, not the other way around.

    ❏ Agree   ❏ Disagree

5. I get enough rest each day.

    ❏ Agree   ❏ Disagree

6. I make time to pursue my own interests outside of my children.

    ❏ Agree   ❏ Disagree

7. I do not make it a habit to compare myself favorably or unfavorably to other moms.

    ❏ Agree   ❏ Disagree

8. I am pleased with how my kids use screen time (and how I use it too).

    ❏ Agree   ❏ Disagree

9. I have another mom friend or group I meet with regularly for encouragement and accountability.

    ❏ Agree   ❏ Disagree

10. I pray for my children every day or most days.

    ❏ Agree   ❏ Disagree

11. I have at least one fun moment and laugh every day.

    ❏ Agree   ❏ Disagree

12. I understand my goal is to launch adults, not to raise children who are dependent on me.

    ❏ Agree   ❏ Disagree

Total the number of statements you agree with:

1-4: You are feeling at the end of your rope most days. The scoreboard reads *Kids 18, Mom 2.* To be a happy mom, you will need to start with a few important tweaks, such as seeing yourself as a leader and acting like one. You've picked up this book just in time! You can do this, Mom.

5-8: You are experiencing moderate job satisfaction as a mom. You long to stress less and laugh more. You second guess yourself at times. You are open to new ideas and motivated to be a better mom. Use the concepts in the book to take your mothering to the next level.

9-12: You are doing great! You're building on a strong foundation. There's no ceiling on joy, so you'll be refining your mommy skills and growing in happiness. As you learn what works in your mom life, pass it on to other moms. In giving and serving others, you'll receive even more.

Becoming HEALTHY

A

P

P

Y

Day 1

Big Rocks First

Do not conform to the pattern of this world, but be transformed
by the renewing of your mind. Then you will be able to test and
approve what God's will is—his good, pleasing and perfect will.

ROMANS 12:2

My youngest child, Lucy, was born with some serious hair. By the time she was four months old, it looked like she had stuck her finger in the light socket. Think scared porcupine, replacing the quills with thick black hair. Kramer from *Seinfeld* had nothing on her.

One winter day, I was Christmas shopping through a store's toy section with my little-miss-big-hair riding in the shopping cart. A mom walked past me with her two older kids following her. She glanced at my adorable baby porcupine and then, loud enough for her own kids to hear, said, "It only goes downhill from there."

I wasn't quick enough to shoot back, "Actually, I have two older kids, and I find it gets better every year. Merry Christmas!" She probably wouldn't have appreciated that anyway. In that moment, I learned something important from that Grumpy Mom. I didn't want to become like her. I don't want to have a negative mindset about motherhood that goes something like this:

Just wait until you get married…all the romance will evaporate.

Just wait until you have kids…say goodbye to your life.

Just wait until your kids are in elementary school…hope you like being a taxi driver.

Just wait until your kids are in junior high…they'll turn into aliens.

Just wait until your kids are in high school…they'll hate you!

Just wait until your kids are in college…they'll suck up every last penny.

Just wait until your kids are young adults…they'll come back to live with you.

The Grumpy Mom anticipates disaster around every corner. For her, saying "It only goes downhill from there" wasn't rude. It was a passing comment that flowed out of the reality of her life. When you have a negative mindset, it not only darkens your outlook, it poisons those around you. Remember the Grumpy Mom made her sour prediction with her own children listening to her every word.

Feed a Healthy Mindset

A few days a year, my kids bemoan the rainy-day schedule at school. Instead of going outside for recess, the kids are herded into the multi-purpose room for the torture of what Noelle calls "boring-day schedule." When they hear the forecast of rain, their young faces fall.

Motherhood can feel a lot like rain. Sometimes you're pounded by storms. Other days you're dragging your feet, a slow death by dreary skies of repetition. Being locked up with whiny kids, laundry piles, dishes, and to-dos can seem like "boring-day schedule" over and over again. Yet in the monotony, do you know you can choose to feed a positive mom mindset?

As you fold your laundry, you can say a prayer of thanks that you are not separated from your loved ones.

As you're running errands, you can listen to positive podcasts in the car.

As you're planning your schedule, you can invite the happiest mom you know to coffee.

It doesn't take much to infuse life into the "boring-day schedule" of being a mom. It begins with having the right mindset. In her ground-breaking book *Mindset*, Carol Dweck contrasts a fixed mindset and a growth mindset.[1] Applying her concept to motherhood, if you have a *fixed mindset*, you believe you're wired with certain talents and abilities as a mom. There's not much you can do to change the hand you've been dealt. If you have a *growth mindset*, you believe abilities can be developed through dedication and hard work. This view emboldens you to learn new things and constantly improve as a mom.

Which mindset sounds healthier for you and your children? You bet— the growth mindset. The days ahead are not carved in stone, careening downhill to the grave like the Grumpy Mom would like us to believe. No, according to Daniel 12:3, "Those who are wise will shine like the brightness of the heavens, and those who lead many to righteousness, like the stars for- ever and ever." Now that sounds much better and brighter, doesn't it?

Puzzles and Priorities

My husband, James, does an object lesson for kids we moms can learn from. He arranges ingredients on a table: sugar, sand, marbles, ping-pong balls, a few big rocks, and an empty peanut butter jar. He asks the kids, "Do you think I can fit all these items into the peanut butter jar?" He begins with the sugar, sand, and marbles. By the time the ping-pong balls are added, there is no room in the jar for the rocks.

So he pours everything out, and this time he begins with the big rocks first, followed by the ping-pong balls. Then he pours in the marbles, sugar, and sand. Now it all fits! He explains to the kids when you put the big rocks in first—things like praying, reading the Bible, doing chores, finish- ing homework—then you have time for the extras in life like riding bikes or watching movies.

As moms, we need to put the big rocks in first. We can put out fires and respond to texts, which seem urgent at the time, while ignoring what's truly important. Slowly, we grow complacent toward Bible reading. We place our children ahead of our spouses. We let our health slip.

What does every flight attendant instruct us to do? Put on your oxygen mask before assisting others. Mom, don't ignore that oxygen mask dan- gling in front of you. Take care of yourself so you can care for your family. Making healthy choices isn't selfish.

Notice the motivation. You don't take care of yourself to escape or look gorgeous for your selfie. You do it to serve others. Putting the big rocks in first involves determining what's really important as a mom. Legendary basketball coach John Wooden says,

> Take a moment and draw a circle around the following personal
> characteristics that you possess: confidence, poise, imagination,

initiative, tolerance, humility, love, cheerfulness, faith, enthusiasm, courage, honesty, serenity.

I hope you circled them all because all are within each of us. It is simply up to us to bring them out.[2]

Go ahead. Circle the characteristics you possess and underline the ones you want to increase in your mom life. These virtuous characteristics aren't handed out at birth. They are mined by use and effort, the hard work of personal development that the growth mindset encourages. For example, if you'd like to become more confident, you can place yourself in situations that boost your confidence, whether that's singing a solo or joining a moms group.

Adopting new positive attitudes and changing behaviors can be overwhelming. Like working on a one-thousand-piece jigsaw puzzle, you may feel utterly lost and think your efforts are pointless. But how do you put a puzzle together? One piece at a time, starting with the easiest first. Don't try to become more patient, scream less, cook more, finish projects you start, and start a neighborhood Bible study all in one morning. Start with one improvement at a time and then build on your success.

Someday, You'll Be Number Five

If your name is Mom, you're probably the most popular person in the house—or in the world. One child asks, "Mom, where is my homework?" while another says, "I need you to sign this," and yet another screams from the toilet, "M-o-m-m-y!" James likes to say Mommy is more popular than Santa Claus.

Because of this instant fame, we can get our priorities all mixed up. Instead of investing in our marriage or relationship with God, we pour everything we have into the most vocal part of our lives: our children. That's why it's really wise to realize that someday you'll be number five. Allow me to explain from my friend, author, mother and grandmother, Kendra Smiley.

When Kendra's brother-in-law was living his last days on earth because of a brain tumor, it made her take a serious look at her priorities. She knew the right order was God first, then her husband, followed by her kids, work, and other good things like volunteer work. She wrote her priorities on a piece of paper and placed it on her desk. There they sat, but it seemed to make no difference. She remembers cleaning the bathtub, crying out to God, "Please help me understand my priorities because they don't do me any good if I can't implement them." Then God gave her this picture in her mind:

> I was doing a watercolor painting, and the paper was in the upright position on the easel. I thought, *You can't paint this way. Everything is going to drip. You have to have everything flat.* But still I painted on that upright paper with the Lord at the top, and sure enough, He dripped down. Then I painted my husband John and the kids, my work, and my service. I realized that God wanted the things at the bottom to be influenced by everything higher on the list.
>
> Often when we think of priorities, we think of time allotment. So does that mean I should spend eight hours with God and six hours with John? No, that's not how life works. It's about letting God drip down into everything you do.[3]

Here's an example of how Kendra worked out this canvas of priorities in her mom life. She was asked by a prominent ministry eighteen months in advance to keynote a large event. She realized that might mean missing one of her son's football games during his senior year in high school. She called the planner back and asked if she could speak on Thursday instead of the better attended Friday or Saturday. She ended up speaking on Thursday and sitting on the bleachers that weekend at her son's football game. That was playing out what God told her to do while scrubbing the tub months prior. Let the things on the bottom of the list be influenced by everything higher on the list, not the other way around.

Kendra has modeled and taught these priorities to her three grown sons. That's why she's number five now on their priority lists. To her sons, Jesus is first, their wives come second, kids come third, work comes fourth, and finally Mom makes the cut at number five. Kendra laughs and says that's hard because her adult kids are still third on her list, but she's number five on theirs! But she's quick to be grateful for the number five spot. She says mothers who insist on being higher in the pecking order usually don't end up even in the top ten.

So remember when you're trudging through a "boring-day schedule" or your ears hurt because of the constant screeching of M-O-M-M-Y, better days are in front of you. After all, it doesn't all go downhill from here.

A Word for Stepmoms from Laura Petherbridge

The healthy family is God first, spouse second, child third. But when a death or divorce occurs, the child moves up a notch on that ladder. If you remarry, the children have to go back to third place. That's a hard transition and many single parents aren't ready to move their child into that position. I advise single parents not to remarry unless they are ready to put the new spouse in the number two spot. That doesn't mean you don't stick up for your children if your new spouse is treating them poorly. It means you have to be prepared for your marriage to take precedence. That's extremely difficult for a mom to do when the children have been in that number two spot for any length of time.

In a first time marriage, children view affection between mom and dad as security. But in a second marriage, it stirs up insecurity because that parent is being taken away. Here's a tip that most parents don't think about: spend time alone with your biological children after you remarry. This will go a long way in assuring them that you have not thrown them under the bus to take on a new spouse. Be as consistent as possible. It could be breakfast on Saturday mornings or Friday night pizza. This way your child knows he or she gets your full attention for one hour at coffee or whatever works for your family. Tell your child, "I love you. Just because I married Joe doesn't mean I have any less compassion for you. I'm still your mom and that will never change. I will always be here for you."

Today's Energy Boost

Can you identify with the Grumpy Mom who isn't exactly enjoying motherhood? Every time a negative thought pops into your head today, think of two positive thoughts to combat it. Spin doctors usually have a negative connotation, but in this case, spin is good.

Today's Prayer

Lord, thank You for speaking to me today. Help me to adopt a growth mindset. I want to learn how to be a happier and more fulfilled mom. Teach me to be more loving to my family members. Show me what my priorities ought to be and how to put the big rocks in first so You will be glorified.

That Might Not Be Food

"Everything that lives and moves about will be food for you. Just as I gave you the green plants, I now give you everything."

GENESIS 9:3

It all started with a scrumptious Christmas gift unfit for a kid. My seven-year-old Ethan received a package of peppermint holiday Oreo cookies from his cousin. The whole package. For one kid. As a good health-conscious mom, I patted Ethan's head and told him how he couldn't eat the cookies all at once. I would put them at the very tippy top of the pantry, and he could ask for a few at a time. By the way, did I mention that peppermint Oreos are my favorite?

Ironically, Ethan has incredible self-control and I apparently do not. For several days after Christmas, I would eat one or two cookies. Okay, more like three or four. I rationalized I was saving Ethan from eating all that terrible sugar. Before long, the cookie bag was *empty*. Ethan hadn't asked for one cookie yet, and I was praying he would forget. He didn't.

A few days before Valentine's Day, he asked, "Mom, where are my Oreos from Christmas?"

"I ate them," I answered lamely just above a whisper.

"You ate *my* cookies!"

I quickly and wholeheartedly said I was sorry. Then I made restitution by going to the store to buy another bag, and this time around, I didn't eat one.

Food can certainly be a stumbling block for us moms. With kids and birthday parties constantly in the mix, the house can become a breeding ground for junk food. I remember attending one party that included a piñata stuffed head to toe with KitKats. I must have eaten dozens of Kit-Kats that week. At another birthday party when Ethan was about five, I watched him sitting at the table alone and serious. While all the other kids had begun playing again, he was scraping every last morsel of frosting off his party plate. He was so passionate and focused on that frosting. I thought, *Oh no, he's like me!*

Help, the DingDongs Are Winning

Hannah Keeley is the producer and host of the television show *Hannah, Help Me!*—a reality makeover show for moms. As a mother of seven, she has learned how to turn things around. Within a few years of becoming a mom, she found herself out of shape, tired, and overweight. Hannah set out to do something about it.

> I had a big life to live and I couldn't do that if I was tired and exhausted with a belly hanging over my blue jeans. I started to really take into account what I put inside my body. When I fueled my body with healthy foods, all of a sudden I had more energy. I wanted to eat the stuff that made me feel alive and energetic and happy. There are lots of people with sugar addictions, and we wonder why we're angry and lethargic. Food can be a blessing or a curse, just like anything else in life.
>
> When I look at a HoHo or a DingDong, I don't see anything God made there. I'm sorry, I just don't see it. But I can look at an avocado or apple or slice of whole-wheat bread, and I can see it as something God created. So here's a simple rule: If it's something God made, enjoy it and eat it. Your body will recognize that as food. But it doesn't know what to do with a DingDong. It's going to take that and stick it somewhere in your hips or thighs. It doesn't know what to do with it![4]

Unfortunately, I think my beloved frosting falls under the category "food God did not make." I love Hannah's humor and the simplicity of her approach. She encourages us to use these three questions as we make eating choices:

- Is this food healthy?

- Is it going to make me feel alive?

- Can I recognize this food as something God made?

Eating healthy requires planning. When we're hungry and on the go, we'll stop for what's convenient. Convenient foods don't usually produce a yes answer to Hannah's three questions. As we wait in line at the drive-thru, we may be planning to order the side salad with balsamic vinaigrette, but we drive away with a double-bacon cheeseburger. It's just too tempting. But we could pack a little cooler with a turkey sandwich and apple to bring with us. Does this take extra effort? Yes. Will it pay off later? Absolutely.

Environment Always Trumps Willpower

My health turning point came for me about thirteen years ago when James's employer hired a corporate personal trainer. James came home with all sorts of new ideas from this walking billboard of physical wellness. I wondered what happened to my chocolate-chip-cookie-loving husband. We traded bagels for oatmeal, sugary snacks for fruit, and we stopped buying ice cream. Within a few weeks of this revolution, my daily headaches stopped. I had so much more energy and I lost a dress size. What began as a trial period ended in a new lifestyle that we both grew to love.

Since making that shift in our eating habits, I've been pregnant five times in my thirties—three babies, two miscarriages. Believe me, I have ebbed and flowed with my nutritional habits (you remember those Oreos). I think the most helpful thing I've learned about losing weight and keeping it off is: Environment is more important than willpower. I can promise myself I won't eat sweets for a day, but when the doorbell rings and I receive a tin of caramel popcorn, what happens? I promise myself that the *next* day I won't eat sweets. Willpower melts away in an environment of tantalizing treats.

During my yearly January ritual of trying to lose the weight gained at Christmas, I just had to have a Dove chocolate. The wrapper read, "Keep your promises, especially the ones you make to yourself." Without missing a beat, Ethan said, "That's funny. If you kept your promise, you might not eat the chocolate!"

Instead of mustering more willpower, we've got to act differently. We need to focus on creating a healthy eating environment so we can have more energy as moms. We may not have control over our work environment or what's served at our friend's house for lunch, but we do have a say about what we stock in our own home. We need to have ready-to-eat fruits and vegetables available in our refrigerator. We shouldn't go grocery shopping when we're hungry, and before we put anything into our cart, we should ask Hannah's three questions:

- Is this food healthy?
- Is it going to make me feel alive?
- Can I recognize this food as something God made?

If you want to lose weight or maintain your weight, start by eliminating from your grocery cart foods that pose a danger to your health. You know your land mines: salty or sweet, chips or cookies, ice cream or cakes. Remember, if you have easy access to junk food, you will get to it. So you want to put roadblocks—big ones—between you and the DingDongs. You can put your junk food in a big box and seal it up with shipping tape. Open it back up at a certain date or when you reach a goal weight.

You can ask your family to join you in eating healthy for a certain length of time. I know, you may echo the words of Erma Bombeck: "In general my children refuse to eat anything that hasn't danced in television."[5] Maybe for one month (or even one week), you could give up soda, dessert, or chips. Most likely you'll see a positive difference during this trial period, and you may decide to adopt some new eating habits as a family.

After binging on Christmas cookies, our family skipped dessert and sugary snacks and drinks for one month until Valentine's Day. At church, Lucy was offered fruit punch. In her little voice, she asked if the drink had sugar. "Oh, that will be a problem," she said dryly. Even our youngest kids can get on board!

I have a friend who used to have two liters of Coke and a bag of chips on hand at all times. After being diagnosed with cancer, my friend had to completely change her diet. You can't find any Coke or chips at her house anymore. Her health is too important for that.

When we moms start eating healthy, it's very likely our kids will follow suit. Hannah's ten-year-old daughter recently said to her, "I'm hungry. Can I sauté some quinoa and spinach?" I know, mine haven't said that either, but it's something to shoot for.

Plan for POWA!

Two-year-old Lucy walked toward me dramatically, shoulders slumped. "Are we going to have lunch soon?" she asked. "I need more POWA!" As moms, we definitely need more "powa" to keep up with active children. Part of that power comes from eating healthy foods that fuel us and make us feel good, not sluggish. We have a wide range of foods to choose from. Just look at the verse at the top of today's reading and you'll see that God gave us a wide variety of plants, fish, and animals to choose from for our nourishment and enjoyment.

Yet so many moms struggle with weight gain, and no amount of dieting seems to help. One of my favorite speakers, the late Zig Ziglar, said that "many people are poor learners because they focus on acquiring more knowledge instead of applying what they already know."[6] We'll buy the next diet book promising a new solution, but we still haven't changed the behaviors challenged by the last book we read.

We all understand that if we eat more calories than our body uses, we'll gain weight. We know that french fries are less healthy than string beans. But we have trouble connecting knowledge to behavior; we'll still choose the french fries over the string beans. Using the principles Noelle and I are learning in *The Compound Effect*, let me show you something small and revolutionary that any mom (and that means you) can do to radically improve her health and happiness.

Let's say Sara the Mom takes the small step of cutting 125 calories each day, and Martha the Mom takes the small, all-too-easy step of adding 125 calories per day. At the end of ten months, there's not much difference in their physical appearance. But by month thirty-one, the difference is apparent. Sara has lost thirty-three pounds and Martha has gained thirty-three pounds. If they started at the same weight, that's a sixty-six pound difference between them, and it all started with a mere 125 calories per day.

See how that small daily habit made such a powerful difference in the health of those moms over time? Whether it's cutting out a donut or adding in an apple a day, the small things you put in your mouth will make a big difference in your energy level and happiness. Need more "powa" in your life? Pick real food to eat at your next meal. And maybe it's not a bad idea to wrap your son's Oreos in duct tape so you can't get to them.

Eight Super Foods for POWA!

- blueberries
- black beans
- spinach
- yogurt

- tomatoes
- carrots
- oats
- walnuts

Today's Energy Boost

What 125 calories can you cut today? (Hint: don't cut out fruits or vegetables.) Make a conscious effort to avoid those extra calories. See, that wasn't that hard!

Today's Prayer

Lord, it says in the Bible that a person without self-control is like a city with broken down walls. Help me to have self-control in my food choices. Holy Spirit, be my comfort and stress reliever so I don't have to go to food for those things. I ask for Your strength to make healthy eating choices today.

Day 3

Don't Stop Moving

Rebekah came out with her jar on her shoulder…She quickly emptied her jar into the trough, ran back to the well to draw more water, and drew enough for all his camels.

GENESIS 24:15,20

I went to a café created just for moms. There was a colorful playground inside, an exercise room for mommy-and-me classes, and small round coffee tables for moms to chat. I struck up a conversation with another mom while my kids went down the slide. They were probably one and three at the time, and I was craving adult conversation.

I asked her about her hobbies, and she immediately lit up. Her passion was playing in a volleyball league.

"When do you play now?" I asked.

"Oh, I haven't ever since I became a mom."

This sounds awfully familiar doesn't it? When we become mothers, many of our interests are put aside for a season or much longer. Sometimes this can't be helped, but when it comes to putting off exercise, we would be wise to get back in the game as soon as possible.

Exercise not only keeps your waistline from expanding, it boosts your mood and immune system, lowers your stress level, and helps you get a good night's sleep. One study showed that depressed adults who took part in aerobic exercise improved as much as those treated with antidepressants.[7] Exercise can help you become a much happier mommy. Yet many moms find it hard to set aside the time for exercise. I imagine women in the Old Testament, like Rebekah in the verse above, got plenty of exercise in everyday life: fetching and carrying water, walking wherever they went. The modern mom revs up the SUV instead.

Find a Family Member to Kick

Being Chinese, I had my share of kids teasing me in school, "Watch out for Arlene! She knows karate!" I hated that. Even James has teasingly introduced me to others saying I had a black belt. I'm always quick to say I bought my black belt at the store. But this year, much to my surprise, we have turned into a martial arts family.

It began when James noticed a boy at school twist Noelle's arm behind her. The boy didn't do it maliciously, but she couldn't get out of his grip. The next thing I knew, James was visiting every martial arts studio within a twenty-mile radius. Our children were going to learn how to defend themselves! He came home one day with a Cheshire grin on his face. "Guess who's starting martial arts?" he asked. "We all are!"

Turns out the studio said we could pay for three kids, and James and I could come to classes for free. So there we were, all five of us in the kids' class wearing black T-shirts with a dragon on the front and matching black pants. All the other parents sat in the waiting area watching, while James and I were the tallest "kids" in the class.

Have I had my share of embarrassment? Sure, like every class when I do the splits and there's about three feet of air between my legs and the ground. Have I wanted to quit? Yes, like when my head was sandwiched under my husband's bent leg as he did the Mixed Martial Arts move known as the "triangle choke." It requires a measure of humiliation to be matched up with a twelve-year-old girl in wrestling and lose. My kicks lack "powa" and wrestling is like calculus. Oh, and have I mentioned that on Fridays we put on full sparring gear? Helmet, chest protection, shin guards, boxing gloves. I either get pounded by James or hugged by Lucy.

But I've found that humiliation is good for my ego. The benefits far outweigh the negatives. As a married couple, James and I have a mutual activity, lots of inside jokes, plus a built-in exercise regimen. Our kids will always remember that we *joined* them instead of *watched* them. This sport adds quality time to the family. Believe me, it's camaraderie with a capital C.

Martial arts works for our family as a physical activity. What will work for yours? I don't expect you to lace up soccer cleats or pick up T-ball. But choose something you can do to make physical activity a regular part of life for you and your kids:

- Ride bikes
- Take long walks on the weekends
- Learn how to in-line skate or ice skate
- Jog together
- Do exercise videos

I encourage you to harness the power of exercising with a family member or friends. For ten years and counting, my mom and I have attended a cycling class together on most Thursday mornings. There's no way I would have kept spinning on my own. Case in point: I think I've ridden the stationary bike we have at home maybe twice in five years. But when I'm motivated to get my mom there, and afraid of my instructor's wrath if I don't come, I get on the bike every week without fail. That's the power of having an exercise appointment with someone else. Just like in eating, environment is stronger than willpower. You may *want* to exercise but you really *won't* until your environment demands it (and when you've paid for it).

Do Sweat It

James is on a pro-sweat kick. "I think you could bottle it up and sell it as a vitamin," he proclaims. "That's gross, dear," I reply. Yet doctors agree there are many positive side effects to sweat. Working up a sweat can ease soreness and pain. According to James Ting, MD, "Exercise stimulates neurochemical pathways in the brain, resulting in the production of endorphins that act as natural painkillers."[8] Sweat flushes out toxins, controls mood swings, prevents colds and other infections, and can even clear zits. So the next time you have the blahs, you might want to sweat it out for thirty minutes. Chances are, you'll regain a sense of well-being and have more energy afterward.

It doesn't matter if you like to bike, walk, run, lift weights, dance, or swim. The point is to keep moving and to find something you will actually do, not just intend to do. You don't need another good idea. You need a habit. According to the "Physical Activity Guidelines for Americans" released by the US Department of Health and Human Services, adults need at least:

2 hours and 30 minutes (150 minutes) of moderate-intensity aerobic activity every week or 1 hour and 15 minutes of vigorous-intensity aerobic activity. Aerobic activity should be performed for at least 10 minutes at a time, and preferably spread throughout the week.

Muscle-strengthening activities that are moderate or high intensity and involve all major muscle groups on 2 or more days a week.[9]

If you're thinking, *How can I meet these guidelines with my schedule?* remember you can spread your activity throughout the week. You can lift weights while watching television, or walk your kids to school instead of driving. Our family does a "magic minute." The five of us will lie down on the carpet, the timer starts, and we'll see who can do the most sit-ups in one minute or hold a plank for the longest. It's fast and fun.

Don't feel bad about scheduling time in your week for exercise. Your kids won't suffer because you went to a fitness class or lifted weights in the living room while they were doing homework. On the contrary, they'll see a mom who takes care of her body, and it will teach them to do the same. Catching good habits from you could make a huge difference in the future health of your kids.

The truth is you'll either make time for exercise now, or you'll take time for appointments with a primary care doctor, cardiologist, and pharmacist later. I'm sure you know other moms who have chronic medical problems that would be greatly aided or eradicated by exercise and proper diet. Fitness guru Jack LaLanne said that exercise is king and nutrition is queen.[15] Get those two things managed well and you'll enjoy a longer, happier life.

You don't have to be athletic in order to exercise. Just let my awkwardness inspire you. I was a five-foot-ten high school girl who couldn't play basketball. I rode my bicycle into a parked car. I loathed anything involving wheels and my feet. I was always picked last for any team. I was terrified of touching the ball in any sport. I've never done a cartwheel—ever. If someone like me can exercise, anyone can.

So now that you are stripped of your excuses, what's it going to be? How are you going to make exercise a habit in your mom life? Remember to make incremental changes instead of promising to go to the gym every day and then quitting after two weeks. You can do this, Mom.

I sure hope that mom from the café is on a volleyball team again. I think it would infuse a lot of joy into her parenting. I imagine her kids would cheer her on from the stands and someday follow in her healthy footsteps.

Easy Exercises for Busy Moms

Squats—Feet hip-distance apart, toes facing forward, bend your knees and then stand up. Keep your weight in your heels and keep knees over toes. If you have a baby, you can use him or her as extra weight.

Chair dips—Sit on the edge of a chair with hands next to your hips. Slide your bottom off the edge and bend elbows to ninety degrees. Keep your back close to the chair and push back up.

Plank—Place your forearms on the ground with your elbows below your shoulders. Press toes into the floor and squeeze the glutes to stabilize your body. Your head should be in line with your back. Hold the position for twenty seconds. Rest and repeat.

Supermans—Lie on your stomach with arms and legs extended. Keeping your arms and legs straight but not locked, lift your arms and legs toward the ceiling to form a long U-shape with your body. Your back is arched and arms and legs lift several inches off the floor. Hold for two to five seconds and lower down to complete one.

And don't forget classic push-ups and sit-ups!

Today's Energy Boost

Are you getting your two-and-a-half hours of aerobic activity and two days of strength training? What is one thing you can do this week to add exercise into your routine?

Today's Prayer

Lord, I know my body is the temple of the Holy Spirit. I want to take good care of it. Show me how to exercise more regularly and effectively. Help me not to be lazy, but instead help me to keep moving and to be healthy for my kids.

Mommy Needs Her Beauty Rest

*In vain you rise early
and stay up late,
toiling for food to eat—
for he grants sleep to those he loves.*

PSALM 127:2

Have you ever heard of the cupcake spirit? No, it's not baking legend or culinary prowess passed from one generation to the next. It's the phrase my husband uses to define anything a mom commits to that is over and above what is required.

It all began years ago when I promised to bring snacks for the Toastmasters group James and I were attending. I signed up for cupcakes on the volunteer snack sheet. So the night before our meeting, I was up late baking those promised cupcakes because I didn't have time any earlier. It made perfect sense to me. I was doing it out of necessity. James thought it was a ridiculous use of time.

"Why don't you just buy cupcakes tomorrow morning?" he asked as I fired up the oven well past 10:00 p.m.

"I planned to make cupcakes and that's what I'm going to do!" I said.

Truth be told, I didn't want to make those cupcakes either. I just wanted to go to bed. I'm not a baker or a cook—maybe that's why I had made it so important to make those blasted cakes instead of buying them. I was going to prove to myself and my husband and the world that I could do it! I lost sleep that night, but my Toastmasters group ate my cupcakes. They weren't anything to write home about. In fact, store bought might have tasted better.

Now whenever James hears me volunteering for something he thinks is unnecessary, he bellows out, "Cupcake spirit!" He knows when I am up at night making cupcakes (or whatever else I volunteered for), I will be sleepy and irritable the next day. He doesn't want to pay such a high price for cupcakes and honestly, neither do I.

Permission Granted

When I'm running ragged, existing on little sleep, I am not a happy camper. But if I get enough sleep—and I'm talking about a solid eight hours here—I am even-keeled, productive, cheerful, and much more reasonable to myself and others. Somehow we've bought the lie that it's nobler to do more and sleep less. Go ahead and take a hit on your personal health and survive on a few hours of sleep. You can catch up on sleep later, but your to-do list is now.

But I say, sleep more and be a nicer person. If you ignore your need for sleep for too long, your health and sanity will suffer and so will everyone around you.

My mentor, author Pam Farrel, tends to burn the candle at both ends. She is a go-go-go kind of person. One of the first questions her doctor asked her on a recent visit was about her sleep pattern. She was going to bed after midnight and waking right after sunrise. He told her sunrise was good, but midnight was bad. Everyone needs at least seven to eight hours of sleep to maintain proper health. Pam says,

> God gave sundown and sunrise for a reason. I think when we give ourselves permission to take good care of ourselves, we're happier people. When you have a good night's sleep, problems stay in their right perspective. It's so easy to feel overwhelmed when you're not rested.[11]

You can't mother like a champion if you're scraping by on a few hours of sleep. Someone on the team is going to pay a price for your fatigue. Your sleeping habits affect you and the people closest to you. Some factors, like a crying baby or chronic pain that keeps you up, can't be helped. But many times, it's the cupcake spirit that's keeping us awake at night, whether it's baking them or looking at virtual ones on Pinterest. Author Kendra Smiley reminds us,

For goodness' sake, Mom, take care of yourself and get rest! I hear too many moms say the kids went to bed and then I stayed up until midnight to clean the oven and the kitchen. Stop it! The kids will not remember that your oven was clean. The kids will remember that you were cheerful when the day started.[12]

Isn't that liberating and helpful to put things into perspective? I'd much rather sleep than clean. Kendra also advises getting up one hour before the kids so that mornings aren't filled with hurry, hurry, *hurry!* That's one more reason to go to bed earlier to start the next day well.

Sleep is important to your health for a number of reasons, including:

- less risk of heart disease, heart attack, diabetes, and obesity

- more energy for an enjoyable sex life

- improved memory

- stronger immunity

- better mood

- clearer thinking

Plus, you can lose weight after catching your z's. Researchers from the University of Chicago and Stanford University found a lack of sleep causes changes in hormones that increase appetite. After just two nights of sleep deprivation, their research subjects had a 24 percent increase in appetite and craved high-sugar, high-salt, starchy foods. Sound familiar? Blood analysis found lower levels of the hormone that suppresses appetite and higher levels of the hormone that triggers hunger. The doctor who headed the Stanford study said those who desire to lose weight should put healthy sleeping habits in the same sentence as healthy eating and exercise habits.[13] Doesn't sleeping eight hours a night sound like a wonderful way to curb your appetite?

Prepping for Dreamland

I saw an advertisement for hiking gear that read "Prepare. Endure. Prevail." I smiled because that sounded like a perfect slogan for motherhood. If you want to be prepared for your feisty toddler or troubled teen tomorrow, you begin by getting a good night's sleep today. Don't take on these challenges exhausted, or prevailing will be out of the question.

Yet for many moms, getting a good night's sleep is not as easy as it sounds. According to a National Sleep Foundation survey, more than half of Americans report at least one symptom of insomnia, such as being unable to fall or stay asleep. One-third of us experience sleeping problems every night or almost every night. The two most common symptoms were waking up feeling unrefreshed and waking up several times during the night.[14] Okay, you moms of little ones or teenagers are thinking *no kidding* right about now.

The good news is you can still do something to get a better night's sleep, starting tonight. There are a few dos and don'ts that will help you get your beauty rest.

The Don'ts

Don't drink caffeine late in the day. Caffeine provides a boost of energy and stimulates your brain—not something you want happening before bedtime.

Don't stare at the clock. If you haven't fallen asleep after about twenty minutes, get out of bed and do something relaxing, like reading in a different room, until you feel sleepy.

Don't watch TV in bed. Set a curfew for all your screens one hour before bedtime. The light from TV, tablets, and computers alerts the brain and makes it harder to fall asleep.

Don't pay your bills or do work in bed. Use your bed for relaxation, not for a desk.

The Dos

Do go to bed at a decent hour. Start getting ready for bed nine hours before you have to wake up.

Do dim your lights. Turn off the lights you're not using in the house and dim the lights in your bedroom a few minutes before bedtime.

Do have calming pre-sleep rituals. Establish a routine such as reading a few minutes or journaling before lights out.

Do keep a list handy. Write down those flashing thoughts of to-dos running through your brain. Once it's written down, forget about it. You can jot down your worries too and pray over them before bedtime.

James bought a nifty pen with a little light on it. This way, even if he wakes up in the middle of the night with a pressing thought—"I have to call this person tomorrow!"—he doesn't have to get out of bed or turn on the light. He uses his lighted pen and goes back to sleep.

Having a bedtime routine is just as important for us moms as it is for our kids. My three kids put on their pajamas, brush their teeth, read the Bible, and share highlights from the day. We end with prayers, I love yous, and "Can I get a drink of water?" and other attempts to stall for time. Our personal bedtime routine as moms may look very similar to that, with less stalling and remembering our glass of water ahead of time.

If you go to bed and wake up at the same time every day, it will be much easier for your body to get into a restful sleep pattern. Resist the urge to do social media (or bake cupcakes) before you go to bed. Make your bedroom as comfortable, dark, and quiet as possible.

The Best Way to Wake Up

I've always had a hard time waking up early. If you can't tell from today's reading, I really love and value my sleep. James teases that "I'm great in bed," but he's not referring to our physical intimacy by that comment! My genuine fondness for my pillow and being in the fetal position fights against my desire to pray and read the Bible at the beginning of the day. One thing that has helped this non-morning person is this simple rule: I don't check my email until I have prayed and read the Bible. Bingo. I always check my email, so this rule ensures I'll have some time with God before the day gets away from me.

Speaker, author, and worship leader Gwen Smith is a mom to three teens. I love what she has to say about spending time with God:

> Straight up, it's not about get up at 4:00 a.m. to do it. It's just do it. It's going to look different in different seasons. When we have little kids, it's going to be harder. It's still the most important thing. I see these blog posts, "I'm breaking up with my quiet time." But we will be exhausted and weary unless we're spending time with the Lord. Our strength is found when we prioritize time with the Lord to read His Word, seek Him in prayer, and listen. Even adding five minutes by reading a verse and saying, *Lord, I'm here. Calm my heart. Prioritize my day. Give me the*

wisdom that I'm lacking. Will You put in my mind the things You want to speak to me today? When we reflect and bring thanksgiving into the presence of God, He unclutters our hearts and makes room to provide exactly what we need. That's the best-case scenario for any mom.[15]

When you awaken from your beauty rest, remember to maximize your day and influence as a mom by seeking God first. Put away the cupcake spirit, lean on the Holy Spirit, and dim the lights early tonight for a good night's sleep. After all, you need your beauty rest, and your kids need a nice mom in the morning.

Today's Energy Boost

What's one idea you will take away from today's reading to get a good night's sleep starting tonight?

Today's Prayer

Lord, I'm here. Calm my heart. Prioritize my day. Give me the wisdom that I'm lacking. Will You put in my mind the things You want to speak to me today? Thank You that it says in Psalm 127:2 that You are waiting to grant sleep to those You love. I can sleep in peace because no matter what is happening in my family, You are in control.

Day 5

More Vitamin G

Oh, that men would give thanks to the LORD for His goodness,
And for His wonderful works to the children of men!

PSALM 107:8 NKJV

What if there were a vitamin you could pop into your mouth to cheer you up instantly? My fun friend author Rhonda Rhea suggests such a thing may exist. Every mom should hide a bag of chocolate chips in the tippy-top of the pantry where no child can reach. Then she can take those suckers like vitamins. Whenever you have a little challenge, just pop a chocolate chip!

I'm afraid that's advice that too many of us are already taking. Since popping chocolate chips gets fattening fast, how about an alternative? I propose popping a vitamin G. Not G as in grumbling, which seems to be a common supplement in the average mom's diet, but G as in *gratitude*.

Moms in Prayer founder Fern Nichols grabbed her morning smoothie and rushed to her car. As she went to open the door, she dropped her smoothie and it splattered on the sidewalk. She faced a choice: would she grumble about it or would she find a reason to be grateful? She decided to give thanks in all things, even spilt smoothie.

> I said, *Thank You, Lord. Thank You that I have the stuff to make a smoothie. Thank You that I can clean it up.* That might sound trite, but it's the little things in life that slip you up and make you a grouch and a grumbler. Then, boy, aren't you fun to be around? How is my smoothie going to affect my day? It's not going to harm my day at all because I choose to give thanks in it.[16]

It's a lifelong learning process to become a person of gratitude. We are commanded to give thanks in 1 Thessalonians 5:16-18, "Rejoice always, pray continually, give thanks in all circumstances; for this is God's will for you in Christ Jesus." Giving thanks puts you under the protection and blessing of being in God's will. Simply said, it keeps your mother heart light.

I Can't Find My Shot

Life is filled with hits and misses. For instance, when Ethan was seven, he enjoyed a particularly amazing day one weekend. He saw his children's pastor get a pie in her face to raise money for missions. He had friends over to play. He went on a special date with his grandparents to his favorite hamburger place. There was much to be grateful for.

Monday was a different story. He didn't go to recess because it was raining. He didn't like the movie showing in the multipurpose room. He scored poorly on his math minute. After school, we went to the library to pick up his books, but I messed up the date and they were no longer on the hold shelf. He cried.

After dinner, I shot hoops with him in the driveway in an effort to cheer him up. We played horse. I won. We played again and I won again. "I can't find my shot," Ethan said miserably. The day ended on yet another sour note. I opened up a new pack of toothbrushes. Noelle picked blue, leaving red for Ethan. "Blue is my favorite color," he whispered.

We've all had bad days like that—sometimes strung together for months! There are repeated moments in motherhood where you just can't find your shot. Every effort is a miss. Your discipline doesn't work. Bedtime rules were bent yet again. Your oldest child is having trouble with bullying and it turns out *she's* the bully. Another child isn't doing homework. How can you be grateful when your home life seems out of control?

Don't wait for a more idyllic time in your parenting to pop a Vitamin G. Gratitude is your secret weapon to immunize your heart from troubles, squabbles, messes, and worries. If you can find the good in the now and give thanks for it, you will trade anxiety for peace. Foolishness for wisdom. Shortsightedness for perspective.

The verse at the top of today's reading about giving thanks to the Lord for His goodness and wonderful works is repeated in verses 15, 21, and

31 of Psalm 107. That repetition urges us not to forget. It's so easy to take things like running water or a warm bed for granted and forget the ways God has provided for our family in the past.

You can start by giving thanks simply for *being* a mom. While Noelle and I were doing dishes, I told her about our struggle with infertility. "Did you know that Daddy and I had a hard time having children?" I asked. She didn't, so I shared with her how I couldn't get pregnant for a long time. I had surgery to remove a fibroid from my uterus, and then the Lord gave us Ethan. Sadly, that pregnancy was followed by a miscarriage at twenty-six weeks, but a year later Noelle came. Then I had another miscarriage and finally our lastborn, Lucy.

I'm sure many of you have experienced a miscarriage or another sorrow on the way to parenthood. If you continually put the emphasis on your disappointments in motherhood, you will naturally find much to grumble about. A bitterness and sadness will settle into your life. But if you constantly highlight the faithfulness of God, you open the door to God's love, joy, and peace to flow through your life. That's solid motivation to choose gratitude in both the big and small things.

The Gratitude Train

One summer we were visiting the Virginia War Museum when Ethan exclaimed, "Look, Mom, it's the Gratitude Train! It was given to the US by the French filled with gifts to say thank you for sending aid following World War II."

Turns out my young history buff had read about the train in a magazine. The Gratitude Train, or Merci Train, was a train of forty-nine French railroad boxcars filled with tens of thousands of gifts to show appreciation for more than seven hundred American boxcars of relief goods sent primarily by individual Americans in 1947. Each of the forty-eight American states at that time received one of the boxcars and the forty-ninth car was shared by Washington DC and the Territory of Hawaii.

Standing there looking at the Gratitude Train with Ethan, I realized what a beautiful picture it would be to have a home with a gratitude train running steadily through it. A constant flow of thanks running between spouses, between parents and children, between siblings (wouldn't that be nice?), and between us and God.

But I must admit, in the midst of endless shouts of "Mommy, come here!" and "Mommy, I need you!," I can feel like grumbling down the tracks of life, not giving thanks. I'm overwhelmed and irritated instead of overwhelmed and grateful. Motherhood is certainly about serving little people with big needs. The Bible outlines what our attitude should be as we labor in our homes. First Peter 4:9-10 says, "Offer hospitality to one another without grumbling. Each of you should use whatever gift you have received to serve others, as faithful stewards of God's grace in its various forms."

In mom lingo, that means pour milk with a smile. Do laundry without complaining. Make your children feel secure at home and enjoy their company. Don't grumble as you serve or rack up points in your mind of what a great mother you are. Banish the mom martyr mentality. Realize your hospitality is your reasonable service to God and your family. God will pour joy into you as you are a good steward of the many gifts you have been given.

Get into the habit of finding things throughout your day to be thankful for. Look for evidences of God's hand in your family. Notice the big and small with wide-eyed wonder and thanksgiving. Recapture that gratitude that flooded your whole being when you held your newborn to your chest. Now that newborn may be a five-foot-three eating machine who says two words all day to you. Nevertheless, you can still give thanks for something.

One night, Ethan and I were playing *Yahtzee*. Luck was on his side because he rolled not one but two Yahtzees, a small straight, a large straight, and all the bonus points he could possibly get. He was so excited to dominate the game and roll exactly what he needed time and time again. The boy was on! After the game was over, he kept exclaiming, "I just can't get over it! I just can't get over it!"

I photographed that moment of joy in my mind. What if we could go through life as moms and consistently think, *I just can't get over it! I get to mother these kids! I get to be married to this man! I get to live in this town! I get to be a part of this mom's group!* What a difference between living life saying "I get to" and "I have to."

Now I know you don't roll a Yahtzee every time you play. Some days you don't experience even one event worthy of an exclamation point. But as Benjamin Franklin says, "Human felicity is produced not so much by great pieces of good fortune that seldom happen, as by little advantages that occur every day."[17]

When you get enough Vitamin G in your diet, that attitude of gratitude will dramatically change your perspective. All of a sudden, you'll find your smile again. The Gratitude Train will run steadily through your home, right on schedule, changing all who live there for the better.

Today's Energy Boost

Write down five specific things you are thankful for about your children:

1. _____

2. _____

3. _____

4. _____

5. _____

Today's Prayer

As it says again and again in Psalm 107, I give thanks to You, Lord, for You are good. Your mercy endures forever. You satisfy the longing soul, and fill the hungry soul with goodness. Oh, that we would give thanks to You for Your goodness and for Your wonderful works to the children of men.

Day 6

Fear, Anger, Stress, Oh My!

"See, LORD, how distressed I am!
I am in torment within,
and in my heart I am disturbed."

LAMENTATIONS 1:20

James and I were attending Dave Ramsey's Financial Peace University when a not-so-peaceful thing happened. On my way out of the restroom, I read a sign that said, "If you're not using the lights, please turn them off." I thought I was alone, so I flipped the switch. Before the door shut behind me, I heard a shrill, fear-filled scream from inside the bathroom. It sounded like a young girl.

I hurried back in and turned on the light. "I'm so sorry," I said to the apparently occupied stall. "I didn't know you were in here." I thought about that little girl's scream for a while. The feeling of her fear lingered with me.

Are there things about motherhood that scare you stiff? Toddler tantrums, potty training, boyfriends, girlfriends, and paying for college come to mind. There are a lot of things for a mom to be afraid of. You can worry about the distant future or about what will happen in the next minutes. You can agonize about school assignments, questionable friendships, and stranger danger.

Many scenarios we fear as mothers are not really motivated by any clear or present danger. We manufacture them in our minds, like the time I pictured my children being abducted when they took a short walk around the block. Fear can muddle your thinking, keep you from using your gifts, and cheat you out of peace. God knows we all struggle with fear. Maybe that's why the Bible tells us more than three hundred times not to fear. In fact, "Fear not" is the most frequently repeated command in the Bible.[18]

We can fear the inevitable disappointments in family life. Your son might not make the basketball team. Your husband could be laid off. Your daughter's BFF may find another BFF. Karol Ladd told me about her friend who has five children, four of whom are boys. When she recognized life wasn't going to be perfect and go according to plan all the time, she started saying to herself, "Oh well." That became her little go-to phrase. Instead of succumbing to fear or frustration, she came to terms with her daily reality. She trained herself to be flexible and to respond with "Oh well" instead of "Oh no!" Karol comments,

> We've got to recognize that life isn't perfect. People aren't perfect. I think a healthy, happy mom has to take that picture of perfection off the wall and throw it away. Yes, we want to strive for excellence and do things well, but life is not going to be about having every duck in a row. We need to be okay with that. Often we want things perfect because we want safety and control. We can make our plans, but the final results are up to God. A happy mom is one who has her eyes on a perfect God. She trusts Him and relaxes.[19]

Be the 15 Percent

Yet it can be so hard for us to trust in God and relax. Dr. Arnie Cole, CEO of *Back to the Bible* and author of *Unstuck*, surveyed more than seventy thousand Christians in America. Can you believe 85 percent of those surveyed said they were defeated by temptation and life-controlling problems, which caused them to struggle alone and give up spiritually?[20] Wow, 85 percent is an overwhelming majority. My guess is that 85 percent of you reading this book can relate to feeling defeated at times. You may be stuck in fear, anger, worry, or anxiety.

The good news is you can become more like the 15 percent surveyed who weren't living in defeat. With deliberate action, you can root out negative patterns in your life and replace them with more positive thoughts and behaviors. Karol Ladd reminds us that anytime you weed something ugly out of your life, you have to get to the root cause.

Ask yourself, why am I so bent on this kind of anger or bitterness? What are the trigger points that are making me spill over? Ask God to show you how to pull the weeds out of your life. It's important to recognize that for every negative quality, there's a positive quality that can replace it. Memorize verses that build truth into your life. Instead of caving into frustration, despair, and anger, you can learn to look up and say, "What would the Lord have me to do in this situation?"

Every mom is going to experience anger. Your time isn't yours when your children are young. There are endless demands and little people pulling on your shirt and stepping on your toes. That's a recipe for just a tad bit of anger to come out. Karol has a helpful formula for controlling anger using the acronym STOP.

S—*Step away from the situation.* When you feel like you're going to explode, step away from the situation. Step into another room if you can. If you're in the car or the store, think of a different place in your mind. I (Arlene) suggest Hawaii.

T—*Take several deep breaths of fresh air.* As you breathe deeply, it physically relaxes your body and gives your emotions a moment to calm down.

O—*Objectively look at the situation.* Often when you're about to fly off the handle, something has triggered it. Your adrenaline starts pumping and you're not able to think as clearly. Maybe you're angry because you're hormonal or hungry, or your husband upset you earlier. Maybe you're angry for reasons that don't have anything to do with your children.

P—*Pray to your heavenly Father.* Recognize you have the Holy Spirit to keep you from sinning in anger. When you don't feel like you have enough control, you can look to God and ask Him to give you grace and peace.[21]

The next time you feel anger bubbling up inside, STOP and use these four principles to calm down. No doubt your conflicts will go smoother with less yelling and more grace.

Get in Community

Whether you are an introvert, extrovert, or a mix in-between like me, you need to be in some kind of community. Motherhood can be a lonely profession. I know many women who left the workforce to become a mom, only to find the days eerily lonely. When you meet a new mom, take a moment to ask a few questions. You might be the bridge between that lonely mom and another woman who may share common interests.

Recently I was at a birthday party for one of my child's classmates. A nicely dressed woman came my way and said, "I don't know if you remember me, but I met you years ago at the library. You told me about a mom's group. I wanted to let you know I joined and it made a huge difference to me, and I wanted to thank you." I was glad I had made the effort to talk with her during a "mommy and me" reading time.

Hugging a friend or laughing out loud with someone is a natural way to fight stress and anxiety. Social media to a degree can meet a need in our lives for connection, but it can't replace physically meeting other moms who understand our life. Laura Petherbridge, coauthor of *The Smart Stepmom*, gives this advice:

> One of the most encouraging things I can say to a stepmom who's feeling like a failure or a total disappointment is that God created us for community. He created us for community with people in similar circumstances. I cannot encourage a stepmom enough to get into some type of a group or event with other stepmoms who understand her pain and loss. At the stepmom retreats I lead, the number one thing moms tell me is I finally feel like I am not alone anymore. I finally feel like I am not the wicked stepmother. Now I have one or two sisters who get it. When they are up, they can help me and vice versa. It's not commiserating; it's not about bashing the biological mom or stepkids. It's getting with a strong group of stepmoms who want their marriage to be strong and thriving and encouraging each other. There is nothing I have discovered that takes the place of that.[22]

Laura's counsel about being in community with like-minded moms rings true, whether you're a stepmom or not. And when making friends, remember the advice of Dale Carnegie, "You can make more friends in two months by becoming interested in other people than you can in two years by trying to get other people interested in you."[23]

I came across this list of "Ten Spiritual Tonics" by Abraham Feinberg. I think it's a wonderfully simple list that summarizes how we can experience emotional health:

1. Stop worrying. Worry kills life.

2. Begin each day with a prayer. It will arm your soul.

3. Control appetite. Over-indulgence clogs body and mind.

4. Accept your limitations.

5. Don't envy. It wastes time and energy.

6. Have faith in people. Cynicism sours the disposition.

7. Find a hobby. It will relax your nerves.

8. Read a book a week to stimulate imagination and broaden your view.

9. Spend some time alone for the peace of solitude and silence.

10. Try to want what you have, instead of spending your strength trying to get what you want.[24]

The more you practice these disciplines, the less room there will be for fear, anger, and stress. Let's be part of that 15 percent who enjoy spiritual health and vitality. As you consider the future of your family, remember the most encouraging command in God's Word: Fear not!

Today's Energy Boost

Read Psalm 91:5-7 aloud and personalize it:

I will not fear the terror of night,
nor the arrow that flies by day,
nor the pestilence that stalks in the darkness,
nor the plague that destroys at midday.
A thousand may fall at my side,
ten thousand at my right hand,
but it will not come near me.

Today's Prayer

Thank You, Lord, that You are my refuge and my fortress. You are my God and I put my trust in You. I know You will deliver me from my fears, anger, and stress. Fill me with Your peace today.

Day 7

Light the Match, Baby

Let him kiss me with the kisses of his mouth—
for your love is better than wine.

SONG OF SOLOMON 1:2

E ven though it's more common for moms to swap recipes than romance tips, the facts of life include sex, even for busy mommies. It's easy to sweep our sexual desires under the rug. There are so many other urgent things to vacuum up first!

To James's utter delight, I met my own love expert while speaking at a conference in New England. Dr. Jennifer Degler is not only a clinical psychologist and author, she is the founder of CWIVES, which stands for "Christian Wives Initiating, Valuing, and Enjoying Sex." How's that for a catchy acronym? Jennifer says when the honeymoon glow fades and the bills and children pile up, we don't initiate sex very often, if at all. We can become sexual slackers, not doing one blessed thing to make our marriage sizzle.

Listen to Your Body

Imagine what it would be like to go three days without food. You'd really be looking forward to your next meal. Your need for food would become paramount in your mind. For many of our husbands, that's how their sexual appetite works. By the time your man has gone without for seventy-two hours, he's thinking about sex a lot. You can help your husband keep his thought life pure by being an all-in lover. I know, some of you are thinking, *Great, but what about me? Why is it always about him?* I'm glad you asked. Here's what Jennifer has to say:

If a woman is thinking I'm doing this for him, eventually that attitude will cause her to lose interest in sex. You need to grab the idea that sex is good for you too. Sex will only be really good for both spouses if it is good for you, not just good for him. So many times as a mom and a wife, we divorce ourselves from being a sexual person. We get all touched out from the kids. Somebody is always hanging on you and needing you. So you distance yourself from your body and from your senses. Sex becomes another thing on our to-do list way down at the bottom.

If you're old enough, you'll remember the successful ad campaign of the 1980s: *Milk. It does a body good.* Moms would be wise to tweak it and think: *Sex. It does a body good.*

We can think of testosterone as a male hormone, which it is, but it's not only a hormone of desire. It's a hormone that produces a feeling of well-being. Men have higher levels of testosterone than women, but women have testosterone too. Testosterone is replenished when you sleep and also boosted with physical intimacy. As you increase your sexual activity with your husband, you'll increase the feeling of well-being in your own body. Did you know sex acts as a natural painkiller and antidepressant because of the endorphins released?

After about ninety seconds of touching your man, oxytocin starts flowing in your brain. That's the bonding hormone you've experienced with your baby. It works to bind a husband and wife together too. The more oxytocin, the more you like one another and build good will toward each other. When you orgasm, it's a fountain of oxytocin. Dr. Degler says it's the glue that holds you together.

Your feelings for each other will wax and wane. There will be days when you're crazy about your man and other days that you tolerate him. Regular times of intimacy stoke the fires of love and, simply put, help a husband and wife like each other more and more.

So how does the busy, touched-out mom prepare her body for more meaningful, fun sex? Jennifer has this advice about getting in touch with your senses:

> Most of the time, we're just trying to get to our dinner. Forget about getting your food hot. We don't really taste, smell, and appreciate what our eyes are seeing since it can be sensory

overload to be a mom with kids all day. We've shut out some senses as a mom—all that touching and those funny smells—then we have to figure out how to awake those senses as a sensual wife. Give yourself a transition time to reconnect with your five senses. When you're in the shower, rub the shower gel on your body. What does that smell like? What does that feel like? Turn on romantic music; otherwise you'll be thinking about something else.

Romance Through the Ages

When your children are young, you may not be sleeping through the night. You're exhausted and constantly covered in someone else's mess. Yet amidst the challenges of the diaper bag days, I love to tell my Mothers of Preschoolers (MOPS) groups, have sex now because your children have no idea what you are doing. If your toddler wakes up early from a nap, and you are having what James calls "mommy and daddy time" behind a locked door, no harm done. She'll knock on your door without a clue to what is going on inside. But as your kids get older, they will begin to wonder! Jennifer says,

> At every stage with your kids, there are different challenges for women sexually. Family life is always changing and moving, and that means the way your sex life works is always changing and moving too. You have to adapt. With babies, you're dealing with nursing. Then in preschool, there is so much lifting. The golden years of elementary school are a busy time filled with activities. During the teen years you're thinking, *Can they hear us?*
>
> I remember when we were newlyweds, we could have sex on the couch. That would definitely scar our kids today! For couples, it's important to adapt your sex life as your children change. Schedule regular time for sex so there's something you're doing that's not mommish. It's womanly. It's an adult thing. You can lose yourself in a mom world if life is all about your kids.[25]

Here are a few suggestions for having more romance through the ages:

Special movie night—When your kids are little, don't let them watch much television. Movie night becomes a main event. Reserve a special video for your kids, and while they watch, you can play.

Sneak it in—If your kids are in school or take a nap during the day, can your husband come home for lunch? Noon is a much better time than midnight for a mom to have energy for sex.

Hire a babysitter—Have the babysitter go out with the kids, if possible, and you stay in. Often after date night, you're too tired to be sexual. But it's a treat to stay in the house without the kids. You can have a babysitter take your kids to the park or to their house if you know the family well.

Leverage the sleepover—If one of your children is invited to a sleepover, figure out a way for your other kids to go somewhere too. It's a great night for your other kids to go to grandmas, an aunt, or good friends to leave you alone at home with hubby.

Take a honeymoon every year—Whether you get on an airplane or drive fifteen minutes away, get away for romance without anyone popping in on you. Check into the hotel at the earliest possible time and stay as long as the front desk will let you.

In his book *52 Things Husbands Need from Their Wives*, Jay Payleitner writes,

> Since we can't count on Hollywood, the media, or retailers, let's take it upon ourselves to reclaim romance for husbands and wives everywhere and hold it up for the world to see. Here's my plan for making marriage sexy again. What if all the committed married couples we know began to hold hands when taking a walk around the neighborhood? Or kissed each other hello and goodbye—even in public? What would our kids think if they saw Mom and Dad giving each other a nice long smooch right in the kitchen? The goal would be to make your third-grader say, "Ewww" or your teenager say, "Get a room."[26]

Moms, it's time to get a room. As I wrote in *31 Days to a Happy Husband*, if you just take from five to thirty seconds a day to give your husband a healthy dose of kissing, you will keep the pilot light lit between you. Remind him each kiss is not the "go" signal. It just means you want to stay connected to have more of what author Pam Farrel calls *Red-Hot Monogamy*. Light the match, baby, because that fire isn't good just for him. It's good for you.

Today's Energy Boost

Take a deep breath and close your eyes. Picture the last time you enjoyed making love to your husband. Smile as you anticipate being intimate again in the next few days.

Today's Prayer

Lord, show me anything that stands in the way of having a great sex life with my husband. Show me the value of intimacy and help me to make time for being with my beloved. Give me a love for my spouse that's like a fire. Fill my body with passion to be alive and to be loved physically by my husband.

Key 2

HEALTHY

Becoming ACTION-ORIENTED

P

P

Y

Day 8

Don't Make Me Count to 100

Those who disregard discipline despise themselves,
but the one who heeds correction gains understanding.

Proverbs 15:32

Remember Fern Nichol's breakfast smoothie that splattered on the sidewalk? My five-year-old Lucy only wishes it was that easy to get rid of her green smoothie.

Every morning, James makes smoothies with various fruits and spinach. Five tall glasses of green yummy goodness. James, Ethan, and I start drinking up (it actually tastes pretty good), but the girls take their sweet time with it—especially Lucy. The girls giggle and chat at the breakfast table as if they don't have a care in the world. This drives me batty!

"Why should I have to tell you again and again to drink your smoothies?" I say for the fiftieth time, my voice and blood pressure rising.

Have you been there before, Mom? You've stared in unbelief as your child did the same thing wrong for the hundredth time. You bellow, "How many times do I have to tell you to…?" Regardless of how much you want to keep your cool, you lose it—again. Kids have an uncanny ability of getting on your very last nerve and stomping on it.

But take heart. The battles will not be won by who can yell the loudest or cry the biggest tears. The war will be won by the smart mom who disciplines not with endless explanations but with action. The happy mom establishes herself as the Leader, not the Negotiator, the Intimidator, or Briber. She engages in what psychologist John Rosemond calls Alpha Speech. Stand up straight when you give instructions to your child and use as few words as possible. Don't bend over to "get on your child's level," as we moms have been programmed to do. When you sound and look like a leader, your son and daughter will (finally) get the message loud and clear.

Less Talk, Less Tone

Dannah Gresh was creating a recipe for disaster. She was going on a road trip to minister to a group of moms and bringing her whole family with her. Her kids were not participating in the car-packing process. Dannah says,

> I remember throwing a fit. I was yelling. I was not mothering or disciplining. I was out of control. At the end of my rant, I screamed "I'm going to count to one hundred, and you'd better start helping." My kids burst into laughter.
>
> Somehow, because I said something so stupid that made us all laugh, I realized that was my moment to reset. "I'm sorry, that was out of control. I ask your forgiveness. Can you please help me?"[1]

You've probably used the words "Mommy's going to count to three…" or maybe you've counted to one hundred like Dannah (her kids still tease her about that today). We can threaten, warn, plead, cajole, and thunder until our face turns red and we feel like exploding. We can lecture our children on the whys and why nots of life. But is this talking getting through? Does our escalating tone and obsession with explaining everything produce more obedient children?

As Dr. Kevin Leman says in his book *Making Children Mind Without Losing Yours,*

> Your children already know what you're going to say. Half the time they can say it *for* you. "Don't be late, you're going to miss the bus." "Careful, you're going to poke your eye out!" "I'm not going to say this again…" But of course you do say it again…and again…and again.
>
> We're tempted to teach with words. "I'll let you go this time, but don't let it happen again." Which do you think speaks louder— the words *don't let it happen again* or the action of letting them go this time? The action wins out every time.[2]

Going back to my girls and their morning smoothies, I realized tone and repetition were getting me nowhere ("You better drink that smoothie or else…"). I experimented with different consequences and worked on my Alpha Speech. Being sent outside alone to finish didn't work very well (they were as slow as ever), but having to change out of a cute outfit worked like a charm for Noelle.

Lucy has been a harder nut to crack. Getting the smoothie for lunch as a consequence or even being served vegetables all day didn't seem to faze her. Yet as I was consistent with some kind of consequence for her unfinished smoothie, she has been doing much better. Proudly, she will show us her empty glass on the rare occasion she beats her sister.

Little kids aren't the only ones who are slow to respond to our instructions. Gwen Smith has a house full of teenagers. With her oldest one driving, she was no longer responsible for the morning ride to school. But as she eyed the clock, she could see her kids were going to be late.

"With the traffic, you need to be gone by now," she said.

"Mom, we're fine. It's going to be fine," her son replied.

They were still eating their bowls of cereal and needing to brush their teeth. They didn't move one iota faster after her comment. A self-admitted yeller and girl of tone, Gwen fought the desire to scream, "You're going to be late! The traffic is going to be awful!" Instead, she gave a simple ultimatum: you can either be out the door now or you can leave your phone on the island. Guess what happened? They left.[34] No amount of ranting or raving would have probably stopped them from lingering over their cereal, but the consequence of going to school without a phone? Whoa, now that's something a teen will respond to.

The Magic Dollar

When I asked moms what made them unhappy, I got answers like:

"I hate it when I have to repeat myself again and again."

"I'm constantly yelling at my kids about their 'forgotten' chores."

"My kids don't do what I ask. They make excuses and argue with me about things they're supposed to do every day."

I can certainly relate to these frustrations. James and I were harping on the kids constantly: "Hang your backpack in the closet." "Put your dish in the sink." "Please help set the table." He was tired of the constant nagging about basic household duties, and he began to brainstorm about the solution. Lean in, moms. The crazy plan James came up with worked like a charm, and it all began with a dollar.

James grew up in an Italian home where the person who shouted the loudest won. He didn't want to yell or get ugly when disciplining the kids. He was looking for a nonemotional, reality-based discipline that would get the kids' attention. One afternoon, he called a family meeting and announced a new rule in the Pellicane household:

> If I have to ask you to do something around the house that's expected, like setting the table, unloading the dishwasher, putting your plate away, or putting your shoes in the closet, you will owe me one dollar. These are reasonable tasks that I should not have to remind you about. If your brother or sister does a task for you because you were lazy, you will owe him or her a dollar. The wages of sin at the Pellicane house is a dollar.
>
> It works both ways. As you do things over and above—maybe you offer to clean up all the dishes after a meal or help your sibling with homework without being asked—you will get a dollar.

About an hour later, it was dinnertime. No one came to help me set the table. One backpack was still in the hallway. There were clean dishes on the countertop that needed to be put away. James called the kids downstairs. "Okay, you all owe me a dollar." You should have heard the weeping and gnashing of teeth that followed. "We didn't know it already started!" they proclaimed. "That's not fair!" they whined. One of them burst into tears.

I was still trying to determine if my husband was a genius or a madman. I immediately thought of that dinner scene in *The Sound of Music* when Maria first arrives and she makes all the kids cry. Captain von Trapp said, "Fraulein, is it to be at every meal, or merely at dinnertime, that you intend on leading us all through this rare and wonderful new world of... indigestion?" I leaned over to James and asked him the same question.

It was a rough start to be sure, but do you know what happened in the days following? I stopped lecturing for the umpteenth time about where the backpacks went. I just said calmly, "Go get me a dollar." As the dollars started draining from their piggy banks, the older kids wised up quickly.

They started unloading the dishwasher. They set the table without being asked. They hung up their backpacks and put away their shoes.

I was flabbergasted at the change. Did my kids change their behavior because they are angelic, kind, responsible children? No, they did it because they didn't want to be flat broke. It's much more fun to earn money than to lose it. We have a desk drawer filled with one dollar bills. The kids know to put their dollar in when there's an infraction and to take a dollar out when there's a reward. These circulating dollars are working magic for the work ethic in our home. Instead of getting a weekly allowance, our kids work by commission. Here's what James says about his magic dollar:

> The beautiful thing about it is that the kids are taking initiative, and we're not nagging them all the time. They realize, "Wow, if I don't giddy up and look for something to do, it's going to cost me some money." I love the spirit of initiative it's putting inside of the children; it's just absolutely beautiful. Any employer would love to see this kind of initiative in anyone. Sometimes they get rewarded with a dollar for their good work, sometimes it slips by and they don't. That's just like the workplace. Sometimes you get a bonus, sometimes you don't. I want my kids to bear the responsibility for basic chores on their shoulders, not on mine or Arlene's.

> When I forgot my lunch as a kid, I forgot my lunch. My mom wasn't going to bring it to me. Many kids today don't have a clue about responsibility because Mommy will bring lunch to school. But when a child realizes Mom is not at their beck and call, that's incredibly healthy for the child as well as the mom. Too many moms are running themselves ragged doing things that children should be doing on their own.

When I woke up one morning and saw my ten-year-old son, dressed and peeling oranges for our family smoothie without being asked, I cannot tell you how satisfying it was to say, "Wow, you're getting a dollar!" Ethan has turned into a "How can I help you?" machine, and I trace the roots of his initiative to good old George Washington. Now that's a dollar well spent!

Today's Energy Boost

Instead of yelling or disciplining with tone, what is an action-based discipline that would work with your children? Could you incorporate the magic dollar in some way?

Today's Prayer

Lord, I give You my mouth. I don't want to nag, yell, or argue today. Help me to discover actions that will discipline my children effectively. Give me wisdom and insights that I don't have. Help me to be consistent in following through on consequences, without anger or malice. Make me into the leader You want me to be. Change my behavior so my children will be better positioned to obey.

Day 9

Prepare for the Next MOMent

There is a time for everything,
and a season for every activity under the heavens.

ECCLESIASTES 3:1

I've heard it said the elementary school years are the golden years of parenting. Your kids are potty trained and sleep through the night. They like you.

When Ethan was in second grade, he and Noelle often biked to school with James, so I rarely drove them. But I cherish in my memory one morning when I dropped off the kids. Ethan hopped out of the car, his huge backpack jostling up and down. He ran about ten feet, and then whipped around, looked at me, and yelled at the top of his lungs, "I LOVE YOU MOM!" Using sign language, he made the sign for "I love you" on each hand. We call that double love. I choked up. Right there in my minivan. I treasured that moment of him yelling in a crowd of his peers, unembarrassed and totally devoted to his dear old mom. I knew that in just five years, he would get out of the car, head toward middle school, and never look back.

But that's okay. Each stage of childhood has a beauty and delight all its own.

I once asked my kids, "If you could go anywhere in the world, where would you go?" Lucy, who was two at the time, answered LEGOLAND, which is less than one hour from our home. Noelle wanted to go to Disneyland and Hawaii. Ethan chose England, Italy, and Spain. What a difference in dream destinations. As kids get older, they think bigger (and more expensive). Their needs, wants, and dreams change through the ages and stages.

I haven't hit those tween and teen years yet, but I've talked to some good friends who have. I am convinced if we moms will take the time to learn about the stage of development that's around the corner for our kids, it will make our parenting journey smoother and happier. Don't listen to the naysayer who says, "Nothing in those books ever helps me. Teenagers will be teenagers. There's nothing you can do about it." That's the "I already know that" mindset that shuts a mom off from wisdom. Instead, lean in and say "Tell me more…I want to be well prepared for what's to come."

Love Slams

While in elementary school, a son and daughter may be involved in the same activities. They both play soccer. They both will make chocolate-chip cookies with you. But as they grow older, they start to be more gender oriented. Hormonal changes will cause a daughter to cry easily and be particularly grouchy once a month. But make no mistake, boys have powerful hormones at work as well. They become more aggressive and assertive.

When Dannah Gresh's son was in middle school, he started body slamming her. She asked her husband, "What's wrong with our son? He's so violent!" Her husband reassured her, "No, babe, those are love slams." So what's a mom to do with these drastically different behaviors in her boy? Dannah says,

> Moms need to be aware that your son will attach to you differently. He wasn't cuddling up to me anymore. His hormones were out of whack. My daughter was crying and my son was giving body slams. My husband explained to Robbie that body slamming would be best done to him instead of me. We redirected that energy into things like banging the basketball against the garage door, which now has lots of dents in it.[4]

Like you, Dannah was interested in learning how to be a better mom through the tween and teen years. She studied Christian leaders such as James Dobson and Dennis and Barbara Rainey. They said the teen years are some of the hardest and rockiest of your child's life, but they can be some of the best if you as a parent become intentional about making them good years.

Dannah's research led her to become preoccupied with becoming a connecting parent. Social science proves the number one reducer of substance abuse, sexual sin, negative peer pressure, and academic failure is parent/child connectedness. Parents who spend regular time connecting with their teens dramatically reduce their risk for harmful behavior.

Knowing that, Dannah and her husband, Bob, did specific things to connect to their kids. Every Thursday night, for example, Bob and Robbie would go to a local sports bar and order a platter of wings. Every week after wing night, Dannah and Bob would have a conversation that went like this:

> Dannah: *"What'dya talk about?"*
>
> Bob: *"Nothing."*
>
> Dannah: *"You were together for two hours. You had to talk about something. Is it that you don't want to tell me?"*
>
> Bob: *"No. We didn't really talk about anything in particular."*
>
> Dannah: *"It's not possible to spend two hours together without talking."*
>
> Bob: *"Yes. It is. We just did it."*[5]

What a great example to us moms that connecting with boys often has little to do with talking. Bob was and is a busy man, and the standing wing night with his son communicated: *You are important to me. That's why I will put you on the calendar as a nonnegotiable appointment.* That connection forged over sweet-and-spicy will not be easily broken.

The Mama Change

A monumental shift happens in middle school as a mom realizes, "Whoa, I don't have the control that I used to have." In elementary school, you may volunteer in your child's classroom or school. You can orchestrate a lot of what happens in your child's world. You know your kid's friends and direct your child's schedule. But as your children grow into teenagers, they become more independent. Our task is to realize this is not a bad thing. It is God's design for your child to grow up and leave your nest one day, preferably before they hit thirty. Your parenting style has to change as your children mature. Gwen Smith says,

> When your kids are little, it's "Don't touch or you're in a timeout." When they're teens, that's not going to fly or else their hearts will shut down and turn against you. We cannot be as hands-on and heavy handed. We need to reason with them and help them understand our thinking process.
>
> You go through the mama change from having a child who wants to hang out with you and hold your hand to now needing space from you. We can choose to have that hurt our hearts or we can choose to recognize when they take those steps away from us, it's actually them beginning that weaning process to be who God created them to be. It changes the way we influence.[6]

As your children grow up, your parenting style should change too. John Rosemond describes the stage between birth and age two as the season of service. Self-explanatory, right? During those years, your child *needs* you to orbit around him or her. But here's the part we often miss. Between the ages of two and three, there needs to be a breaking of that codependency as the mom does less and less for that child. The next stage is the decade of discipling between ages three and thirteen, followed by a season of mentoring to our teens.[7]

What stages(s) are you in now with your kids? Some seasons are naturally more challenging than others as a parent. It's hard for mama bear to respond calmly to rolling eyes, disrespectful tones, messy rooms, and daily drama. As Mark Twain famously advised, "When a child turns 12, he should be kept in a barrel and fed through the bung hole, until he reaches 16…at which time you plug the bung hole."[8]

Staying in God's Word will give you wisdom and patience to ensure you don't plug up that hole. When you feel like screaming, apply a verse like Proverbs 15:1, "A gentle answer turns away wrath, but a harsh word stirs up anger." When Gwen Smith's teenage son leaves his shoes yet again in the wrong place, her natural instinct is to yell, "This is not a shoe collection area!" But with Proverbs 15:1 in mind, she says, "Honey, I know you have a busy schedule. But taking your shoes upstairs will help us. I'm not trying to complicate your life." And guess what? Those kind words turn away anger and move those shoes right up the stairs.

But I Want to Go Back

Years ago when I brought Ethan to the first day of kindergarten, I wasn't just nervous. I was *nerviosa*. I was enrolling my English-speaking son in a dual immersion program where 90 percent of the day would be taught in Spanish. Seeing the kids lining up in front of the classroom, I squeezed Ethan's hand and put on my best game face. "This is so exciting!" I said, halfway serious and halfway wanting Ethan to catch my pretend enthusiasm. But Ethan didn't need any help. He said beaming, "It's so exciting especially for me!"

His teacher made her announcements in Spanish and an assistant teacher translated the necessary instructions in English. We parents stayed with our kids for the first fifteen minutes of class, completing a scavenger hunt together consisting of places like the bathroom, student cubby holes, and the library. When the teacher said "Adios padres!" it was time to cut the umbilical cord. A few kids broke down and cried, but Ethan didn't even flinch when I walked away. He was ready whether I was or not.

Sometimes our kids mature to the next stage before we want them to. I remember a time when Cheerios fixed any and every situation in my mom life. An older mom cautioned me, "In a little while, those Cheerios won't work anymore." I thought she was crazy, but she was right. It's so helpful to have healthy moms in your life who have children older than yours. Just like other professionals, we moms need coaches. Author Janet Thompson says,

> We're building up generations, making a haven, and creating wealth with our finances. So much comes down to us, and if we don't take it seriously, we can do some serious destruction. You need a coach. You've got to have someone building into you. You never stop growing. You never stop learning. You need someone who is about two steps ahead of you, coming alongside you and holding you accountable. You weren't meant to do it alone.[9]

We can't go back to the glory days of Cheerios and cute chubby babies (and those of you who are there right now, don't worry, this too shall pass). Each stage of parenting has a beauty all its own and requires us to understand our children in different ways, even as they grow into adults. Look for a coach who can guide you and cheer you on through the different ages and stages. Maybe that coach is your mom, grandma, aunt, or family friend. Keep leaning in to wise, older mothers and whisper, "Tell me more…"

Today's Energy Boost

What's one thing you can do to learn about the next stage of parenting you will experience? You can take an older mom out to coffee or read a parenting book (I recommend John Rosemond's books) or…

Today's Prayer

Lord, for every season of motherhood I give You praise. You knew my child even before he or she was born. You know everything my children need to grow in life and godliness. Equip me to be a positive mom at every stage of development. Give me grace when I falter and wisdom beyond my own abilities.

Day 10

Whoa, She Really Did Mean It!

A fool spurns a parent's discipline,
but whoever heeds correction shows prudence.

PROVERBS 15:5

The year was 2009 and it was my birthday. What was my simple birthday request? To take family photos in the park. I handed five-year-old Ethan a navy polo shirt to wear.

"*I want to wear something with a car!* I will *not* wear that blue shirt!" he screamed at the top of his lungs.

I told him matter-of-factly that if he didn't get dressed in that navy shirt, he would not get any ice cream cake. He weighed his desire to wear cars and his desire to eat ice cream and chose wisely. "Get dressed, we're leaving in ten minutes," I told him. But ten minutes later he was still running around the house in his underwear.

James told Ethan he would just have to go shirtless all day since he liked being naked so much. But that got *my* attention. I didn't want to have a half-naked boy in my birthday pictures. So James modified the discipline and told Ethan he would have to remain shirtless until we got to the park.

He went ballistic. "I want to wear a shirt! I'm so cold!" He started shivering dramatically. I handed him a blanket. He pushed it away. "Only a shirt will keep me warm!" he whimpered. My structure-and-rules-oriented boy was freaking out because he was going to ride in the car without a shirt on.

When Ethan finally got his shirt back, I told him firmly that if this happened again, he would go shirtless for even longer. This was action-based discipline at its finest. If you want to complain about what you're wearing, fine. You can wear nothing. That certainly did the trick for Ethan. He's never pulled a stunt like that again. Now you may be thinking, *That will totally not work for my child. He would love running around naked all day!*

You've got to create negative consequences that will speak to your individual children. What works for one might have the opposite effect on the other. Rhonda Rhea remembers,

> With one child, I felt like I needed to make a holster with a paddle so I could carry it with me all the time. But I had another child that I could just look at and they would be immediately repentant. Parenting requires being able to read your children. Are we always going to do that correctly? No, but God's grace is much bigger than our mess ups.[10]

Regarding discipline, an underlying commitment is required for the happy and sane mom. Read this out loud: *I will make any behavior I don't want from my child counterproductive.* When your child misbehaves, the consequence will be so swift, sudden, and decisive that your child will think twice before doing it again. For Ethan, I wanted to make it counterproductive to fight me about what he was going to wear.

One of the reasons kids whine so much is that it works. By the tenth time they've asked for that candy bar or video game, we're worn down and give in. Their whining is productive. But what if whining was counterproductive *every* time? What if you said, "Oh, I hear you whining. That means we won't be having any candy today"? And what if you actually meant it?

Consistency Is Your Friend

If you've struggled with being a consistent disciplinarian in the past (and who hasn't), take heart. You can make a U-turn today. I was speaking at a MOPS group and my topic was "Mama's Gonna Win!" After the meeting, one of the moms handed her daughter half a cupcake. The girl demanded loud enough for the whole room to hear, "I want the *whole* cupcake!" The mom calmly replied, "You can have half a cupcake or nothing. I will throw away your cupcake if you are going to cry about it. You need to use your manners." It was a great illustration of what I had just talked about! Unlike most people, moms get to put what they learn into practice right away.

Author and mommy blogger Kristen Welch says this about being consistent:

> Consistency is just so crucial. If we truly want a Jesus-centered home, it takes consistency to not give in to every whim and demand. There are a lot of demands with children. It's so physical when they're little and then it's very emotional as they get older.

Kristen's three children use a chore chart. One of the kids loves to serve, and checking tasks off the chore chart is a breeze. Another child, not so much. When it's this child's turn to do the dishes, Kristen has to ask over and over again. It was getting very frustrating, but Kristen was determined to be consistent and not scrap the chore chart.

> This is what we do as a family. We take turns. I'll never forget the first time my child got up from the table without being asked, checked off the chart, and started cleaning the kitchen. I wanted to cry. Her presence in the kitchen was miraculous. We got to say, "We're so proud of you. We see the growth in you." That was special and meant a lot. The next time it was her turn was even easier.[11]

See how being consistent helped Kristen's child to grow and mature? When you're consistent with your house rules, your children will (eventually) get the memo and grow up as a result. Don't give up early just because you're not seeing any results. Many times moms will quit after a week or two of trying something new like a chore chart. They'll say, "It didn't work for my family." Yet if they would stick in there longer, a helpful new habit would develop.

As a mom, you need to make it as easy as possible for your children to obey your house rules. This involves being consistent because it's awfully hard to hit a moving target. If your child is punished on Monday for doing XYZ, but walks away unscathed on Friday for doing the same thing, it's confusing and frustrating for your child. Inconsistent discipline leads to a lack of respect for your leadership.

Clarity Is Key

Another thing you can do to help your child be obedient is to state the rules clearly. Don't assume your child can read your mind or can practice common courtesies automatically. Here's Rhonda Rhea on rules:

> I'm not a math person, but I do understand if I go down the highway at 70 mph in a 60 mph zone and I get stopped, I can't argue about getting a ticket. I earned it and I know it because I already know the rules. I think we have to be careful in assuming our kids know rules. A lot of times we think, *That's common sense, that's logic.* But it's like taking an alien and dropping them on a new planet. We need to tell our kids what the rules are and then enforce the consequences for breaking those rules. We can't expect them to know rules we haven't told them. I think it's wrong to punish them for breaking rules we never did speak.[12]

One of the spoken rules at the Pellicane household is, "If you don't eat your vegetables at mealtime, you'll see them again at the next meal." As you might guess, that's usually breakfast. Now before you praise me for my superior nutrition, please know that my vegetable servings are pitifully small, probably the size of my third grader's fist. Well, my little Miss Lucy at three years old had a will—and apparently a stomach—of steel.

She had passed on her veggie medley (beets, carrots, broccoli) at dinnertime. Following our stated house rules, she was served those vegetables and the famous green smoothie for breakfast. She continued her strike against the dreaded veggie medley, so she was served it again at lunchtime. She didn't eat a bite. Again, the veggies at dinnertime and she didn't crack. Wasn't she hungry by now?

The kids went to church that night and were served pretzels, cookies, and gummy Life Savers. Ethan told Lucy, "You can't eat that because you didn't eat your veggies!" The teacher told me later that Lucy almost lost it—tears welled in her eyes, but she recovered. She knew it was against house rules to eat anything else until she ate her veggies. A side note that was very sweet: Noelle skipped eating the snack in an act of love and solidarity for her younger sister.

By now, some of you are thinking, *Oh, just let the poor girl eat the cookies!* But remember, if you can be consistent when it's tough and win, your child will learn an unforgettable lesson that will make your future mom life much easier to manage.

The next morning, Lucy stared down her veggie medley. I broke (a little) and sprinkled some cranberries on top of the veggies. I went upstairs to get something, and when I came back to the breakfast table, Lucy had opened the cranberry bag and was having a feast!

I asked her if that was the right thing or wrong thing to do. She said, "Wrong thing." Then, ever so slowly, she began putting those little veggies in her mouth. She finally finished the bowl of veggies and could move on to other food groups. Although Lucy has had vegetables for breakfast more than once since that day, she's never repeated her full-blown hunger strike. She's learning that refusing to eat vegetables is counterproductive and the wrong thing to do.[13]

Today's Energy Boost

When your child misbehaves today, give him or her a swift consequence and be consistent. Don't waver. Make your child think, "Whoa, she really did mean it!"

Today's Prayer

Lord, help me to follow through and be consistent with the rules I give to my children. Give me the physical and emotional strength to outlast and outsmart my kids when I need to. May my words and actions be pleasing to You today. Help my children to respect and obey me so they may prosper and grow.

Day 11

Stop Engineering Your Own Prayer Requests

He who spares the rod hates their children,
but the one who loves their children is careful to discipline them.

PROVERBS 13:24

H ave you ever heard of the broken-windows theory? It's the idea that serious crimes can be reduced in urban areas through the strict enforcement of laws against lesser crimes such as graffiti and vandalism. When buildings go unrepaired, they tend to be vandalized further, inviting more crime into the area. Squatters may settle in and before long, the whole neighborhood goes down. Fixing those first broken windows in a community can prevent the escalation of damage and crime.[14]

What about applying this broken-windows theory to motherhood? If you let your child get by with a few minor infractions, before long those disobedient behaviors become more frequent and more serious. Can I get a witness? But if you clamp down on the first signs of lesser crimes, like sassing back or not picking up toys, you're communicating to your child: "You live in a home of order. Here are the rules you must follow." You're the sheriff in the town and your child is a townsperson, not the other way around.

Unfortunately, instead of addressing behavior issues while they're small, we often overlook them because we're busy, tired, or distracted. We've believed the mantra, "Don't sweat the small stuff." If your child pops a slight attitude, you might think, *Oh, we'll fix that later. Kids are going to have attitudes.* It's like there's a tiny broken window in the home, and you've just let it go. Your child notices that and sasses back more often, so much so that it becomes the norm for both of you. If you don't set the standard with the small things, those small things will build up and escalate. The broken windows take over. Your lack of a response communicates to your child, "Go ahead and do whatever you want. It's a mess in here anyway."

When you don't act as the leader of your home, things begin to fall apart. Stress wipes you out. You end up with a long list of prayer requests for your children. Now obviously, there's nothing wrong with having prayer requests for your child. But some prayer requests can be avoided—if we will correct our children while they are young. As it says in Proverbs 19:18 (NKJV), "Chasten your son while there is hope, and do not set your heart on his destruction." According to the Matthew Henry Bible commentary about this verse:

> Parents are here cautioned against a foolish indulgence of their children. As soon as ever there appears a corrupt disposition in them check it immediately, before it gets head, and takes root, and is hardened into a habit. Do not say that it is a pity to correct them, and that, because they cry and beg to be forgiven, you cannot find it in your heart to do it…your forgiving them once, upon a dissembled repentance, does but embolden them to offend again, especially if it be a thing that is in itself sinful (as lying, swearing, stealing, or the like). It is better that he should cry under thy rod than under the sword of the magistrate, or, which is more fearful, that of divine vengeance.[15]

Although written in 1706, these words are extremely relevant for today's mom. Friends, let's not engineer our own prayer requests because we're afraid or too tired to correct our children. You and I are the neighborhood watch and we must repair the broken windows before they deteriorate into something much worse in the hearts of our children.

Don't Wait, Create

One of James's sayings about parenthood is "Don't wait, create." It's about creating different scenarios that will inevitably happen to your child. Instead of waiting for your toddler to walk out into traffic, you practice on the sidewalk at home how to cross the street. Before going to a nice restaurant for someone's anniversary, you practice table manners at home.

When the kids were small, we wanted to teach them to come when we called. So I explained to Ethan, "When Mommy says come, you need to stop what you're doing and run right over to me. Let's try it!" I would put him on the floor with a bunch of cars. Then I'd walk several feet away and say, "Come to Mommy!" He'd sprint right over because it was like a fun game. I'd hug him and tell him he did a great job. We did this a few times with me yelling "Come to Mommy" from different parts of the house.

Here's where it gets cool. Hours later, I could yell "Come to Mommy!" and he would stop what he was doing and run to me. But as the days passed and this novel game wore off, he started to ignore me. I would say firmly, "When Mommy calls you, you have to come right away." And we'd try it again until he got it right, and then I'd heap hugs on him. We ran this drill regularly at home, and then when we were out in public, I could call for him and he would come.

For younger children, you can create these kinds of drills to keep them safe and you sane. With your tweens and teens, you can continue to create opportunities for learning. Here are a few ideas of things you can practice with your son or daughter:

- How to interact with your teacher if you don't understand an assignment
- How to respond when a girl says something mean to you
- What to do when a boy pushes you
- What to do if you see something inappropriate online
- How to choose clothes that are attractive and modest
- How to interview well for a part-time job

When you're actively involved in teaching your child about sex, relationships, money, and school, you shave off years of your child's education in the school of hard knocks.

Kendra Smiley says, "One of the things that was really helpful to me was this question: What's my goal as a parent? My ultimate goal was to raise a responsible adult."[16] I think we would share that goal with Kendra.

Don't wait passively for life to teach your child lessons. Think of the challenges your child faces today, and create game plans and solutions in the safe lab of your home.

More Margin Please

We engineer our own demise as moms when we take on too many responsibilities. If you're like me, you're always in a hurry. Clock is ticking!

I went to the library with my girls one Saturday morning. It was 10:30, but there was a sign posted on the door: *Closed until 12:00 p.m. for a civic meeting.* I didn't want to wait ninety minutes, but we did have a book on hold. So, we went to the post office and the grocery store nearby. We had plenty of time, so the line at the post office wasn't nearly as annoying as it usually is. I didn't wheel my grocery cart as if it were in a race. I let Lucy dawdle in the aisles. We still ended up at the library before noon, so we sat on a bench and read the books we were returning. It was actually really nice. I realized that perhaps many of the tight deadlines that seem to rule my day are self-imposed. We got all our errands done that day. It took a little bit longer than I would have liked, but the inconvenience made me slow down and enjoy the company of my girls.

We can pack our mom lives and mom days with more than what's necessary. Mother of seven, Hannah Keeley, says,

> I think moms heap a lot of junk on themselves, going above and beyond to do stuff and work themselves into a frenzy. No one said you have to scrapbook every day of your life and stick it in a binder. No one said you have to prepare 365 meals. We heap so much onto our platters because we look on Pinterest and everyone has these beautiful homes and awesome printables. That is ridiculous to think we have to live like that. So we have to figure out, What are we taking on that's just not necessary?
>
> I've seen moms do stuff for their kids that their kids are totally capable of doing. Why is your middle-schooler not doing their own laundry? Any kid that can program a phone or find out how to work the television can figure out a washing machine. They can load a dishwasher.
>
> I don't have a blade of grass in my front yard. I've got wallpaper pulled off in the foyer. But our house is filled with joy and peace

and love. And I'd much rather have that than fresh wallpaper. I'm a professional mom with seven main accounts. I'm majoring on the major stuff.[17]

What parts of your mom life could be pruned back so you can major on the majors? What household tasks could your children do (albeit imperfectly) to give you more free time? When you make more margin in your day, you will be a nicer person and a more effective mom. You can use the same saying for yourself: *Don't wait, create.* Don't wait for life to hand you a less stressful, activity-laden day. Create that day and the caliber of motherhood you want.

Broken windows…beware!

A Word for Single Moms from Laura Petherbridge

There was a time when I was very bitter about marriage. It seemed to work out for everybody except me. I knew I had to do some damage control after that. The last thing you want to pass on to your children is bitterness. Never bash your ex in front of the kids. It's easy to say, hard to do. You've got to look for great role models of marriage for your kids.

Most single moms think, *I have to spend all of my time with my kids. I have to dig in.* It's going to seem counterintuitive, but I say give yourself a break, mom. Go have some fun with your friends. Be with other couples and have great experiences that you can tell your kids about. When I was a single mom, I got sick of being me. I didn't like who I'd become. So I got involved in church, which was tough as a single mom. I kept showing up and coming back. I found a tribe I could be honest with. I told them, "I don't like who I'm becoming. Can you hold me accountable?" Good friends can do that for you and you can do it for them as well.[18]

Today's Energy Boost

What broken windows need immediate attention today? What's one activity you can take off your plate so you'll have more time to address the more pressing need of discipline in your home?

Today's Prayer

Lord, give me the wisdom and strength to discipline and correct my child while there is still hope. May I be a force for good in my home. Use me in my child's life to shape his or her character. Show me how I can slow down and reduce my stress, so I can be more available to major in the majors.

Day 12

Use Your Mommy Guilt for Good

*Let us draw near to God with a sincere heart and with
the full assurance that faith brings, having our hearts
sprinkled to cleanse us from a guilty conscience.*

HEBREWS 10:22

There are days when you feel like a huge failure as a mom. Your house is a mess. One of your kids pushed another kid in preschool. Your older child is having attention problems in school. And you're eating fast food for the third time and it's only Wednesday.

It's easy to fall prey to a victim mentality. *Woe is me, I'm such a loser. So-and-so would never let herself go like this. I'm a terrible mom.* But that negative self-talk doesn't do much to improve your life.

Hannah Keeley remembers as a new mom going over to the laundry basket, catching a glimpse of herself in the mirror, and thinking, *Who is that overweight, exhausted, depressed old woman looking at me?*

> I was boohooing, full on crying. I took my husband's sock and I was wiping my face, blowing my nose, and thinking *I've reached the bottom.* It can't get worse than blowing your nose in your husband's sock. I was just so overwhelmed.

> After a while, I realized no one was coming in to help me. No one was showing up at the door with a big check. No team was coming to my house to clean it up. No one was coming to be my personal trainer. I've seen the movies and someone is supposed to sweep in and fix everything. Fortunately for me, the Holy Spirit did that. I finally realized I was trying to do things

my way and it wasn't working out. I did something that totally changed my life: I started folding laundry. The reason that one act changed my life is I realized if anyone is going to do this, it's going to have to be me.[19]

Instead of letting herself wallow in mommy guilt, Hannah took action and decided to improve her skill set as a mom. She rolled up her sleeves and started folding laundry. That's where she started. Where might you start?

The Difference Between Bad Guilt and Good Guilt

Bad guilt says "I'm no good." Good guilt says "I did something wrong and I'm sorry." Author Philip Yancey puts it this way:

> Guilt is not a state to cultivate, like a mood you slip into for a few days. It should have directional movement, first pointing backward to the sin and then pointing forward to repentance...True saints do not get discouraged over their faults, for they recognize that a person who feels no guilt can never find healing. Paradoxically, neither can a person who wallows in guilt. The sense of guilt only serves its designed purpose if it presses us toward the God who promises forgiveness and restoration.[20]

As it says in 1 John 1:9, "If we confess our sins, he is faithful and just and will forgive us our sins and purify us from all unrighteousness." What a beautiful promise for us imperfect people—moms who make mistakes, like burning granola. Yes, I did that recently when James popped his delicious homemade granola into the oven. He was going to take Noelle out to ice cream for a date. All I had to do was bake it for fifteen minutes and then turn it every five minutes until it was done. Easy enough, right? I was watching *I Love Lucy* with Ethan and Noelle, and you got it, I burnt the whole batch.

When the garage door opened, my heart sank. As Ricky Ricardo would say, I had a lot of "splainin" to do. James was disappointed and wondered how I could have burnt it all. A few minutes later, I was alone in the kitchen washing the dishes. I felt so guilty. I had already apologized, saying, "I'm really sorry I burned the granola and destroyed all your hard work and wasted the money."

"It's not a big deal," James had graciously replied. "It's okay."

I realized I could make myself and my family members miserable for quite some time commiserating that lost granola. I could beat myself up about my mistake or I could move on. The next morning, we did not have any delicious granola to eat. I had to stop rehearsing my failure ("I'm such a lame mom") and simply move on to eggs and toast.

You don't have to be a perfect mom. Cut yourself some slack when the cupcakes fall apart or you feel inadequate compared to other moms. I like what author Kathi Lipp says,

> When did mom guilt become a requirement of being a mother? I think advertisers take mommy guilt and say: You feel guilty about being a working mom—well, here's how you can buy your children's love. You feel guilty because you're staying at home and you can't afford everything—don't worry, you can afford this. They have taken it and run with it to keep you in a place of not being satisfied.
>
> One of the best things we can do with mommy guilt is to accept and love on each other. I think we have set up these social paradigms that say if that person wins, that means you lose. I know a mom who loves making beautiful pastries, but she's scared to bring them to school because other moms will say, "I can't do that. You are making me feel bad." We all have different gifts, and we have to give generously out of the gifts we've been given.[21]

Don't let another mom's success or perfect pastries make you feel like a failure as a mother. You don't have to do things exactly like the moms around you. You don't have to try to duplicate someone else's experience. Drop your unhealthy guilt. Focus instead on the things specific to your journey as a mom, not someone else's journey.

Humble Pie Is Yummy

Your children aren't going to act perfectly all the time. That's an understatement, right? But there is an upside. Here's what author Karen Ehman says:

> The misbehavior of my children keeps me humble. It keeps me going to God for the answers because I certainly don't have them.

If I could be a perfect parent and I never made a mistake, and I never made a bad call, and I always knew the right thing to say and the right time to say it, I pretty much could be my child's everything. My child would have no need for God. So my imperfections, as much as I want to beat myself up for them sometimes, I use as a springboard to point my kids to God.

Don't tether your identity to your child's choices, whether they are good or bad. If you learn to build your identity on your child's right choices, that's a dangerous place to live. It's equally dangerous to tether your identity to their bad choices. If you're responsible for their bad choices, then that would mean you're also responsible for their good choices, and everything good and righteous in my kids is totally because of the Lord, not because of me. Perhaps in spite of me!

Yes, we need to cheer them on when they make good choices and correct them when they make bad ones, but we need to know that their choices are their own. We get that up-and-down emotion of motherhood. "Johnny got student of the month?" Yay, I'm a good mom! The next day, "Johnny got called to the principal's office?" Now I'm a terrible mom. Our identity has to come from Christ and not our kids.[22]

You can wait for your child to humble you—or for your husband or a coworker or friend to humble you—or you can choose to humble yourself first. When you use your guilt to humble yourself before God and cry out "I need Your help!," God will come through for you every time.

When Noelle was three, she loved scribbling on paper while James worked at his desk. She'd bring him what only a parent could call artwork and say proudly, "This is for you, Daddy!" He had a little pile of this artwork and, of course, those pieces of paper eventually ended up in the recycle bin. One day, Noelle gave James one of her masterpieces. He thanked her for it and absentmindedly threw it into the garbage.

"Daddy, you threw it in the trash!" she exclaimed.

"Oh no, Noelle. That's where I keep it—it's a storage place!"

You know what's great about your Father God? He can take your trash and redeem it. He can take your parenting mistakes and teach you lessons that will make you soar as a mother. He can take the bad memories you have stored in your mind and replace them with thoughts of peace and healing. Just begin by admitting freely when you've made a mistake. Receive God's forgiveness and lay down your unnecessary mommy guilt.

Today's Energy Boost

Can you tell the difference between bad guilt and good guilt? Make a commitment to pay attention to good guilt but to dismiss the taunting voice of bad guilt.

Today's Prayer

Lord, I come to You as an imperfect person. Forgive me for the mistakes I have made as a mother. Help me not to sin against You or my children. Show me how to make amends for any wrongs I have not dealt with. May I live in the freedom of Your forgiveness. Thank You for Your grace.

Day 13

Your Game Plan for Screen Time

Teach us to number our days,
that we may gain a heart of wisdom.

PSALM 90:12

I don't need to tell you that screens are part of family life like never before. The average American child between the ages of eight and eighteen spends more than seven hours per day looking at a video game, computer, cellphone, or television.[23] By the age of seven, a child born today will have spent one full year of twenty-four-hour days watching screen media.[24] Yikes!

Here's a key question for the happy mom: Is technology bringing you closer together as a family or is it driving you farther apart? You might buy a giant flat-screen TV so your family can cuddle, bond, and munch on popcorn for Friday movie night. But in reality, one person monopolizes the big screen, while the other members of the house retreat to their own personal screens and spaces to watch different things. Screens can be used to bring families together (like skyping with Grandma), but they are typically used independently, with each family member glued to their own device.

Screens are not the problem; the problem lies in the way we constantly use them. When your child has free time, what's the default activity? For the average family, free time equals screen time. But screen time that's not purposeful tends to be a waste of time and negative influence. Pixels instead of parents take center stage. Children are like wet cement, and nowadays most are being imprinted by screens, not by moms or dads. It doesn't have to be this way.

Choose Your Plan Wisely

When you walk into a cell phone store, you have a dizzying array of plans to choose from. In the same way you choose a cellular plan to suit your family's needs, you need a digital plan for screen use in your home. How much time per day is allowed? Which shows, games, and social networks are approved? Without a working plan, your child's time will erode into mindless screen time and entertainment that usually runs counter to everything you are trying to instill as a mother.

Below are some suggestions to get your brain in gear. Pick and choose what you need—you don't have to replicate anyone's plan, including mine. You just need wisdom to devise the best plan for you and your kids—and stick with it. We'll begin with the Pellicane game plan, otherwise known as "The Dinosaur Plan."

None of our three kids have a gaming device, tablet, or phone. The kids use our laptop for homework, which ends up being about two hours per child per week. When James and I were first married sixteen years ago, he asked to do a no-cable trial period of one month. I agreed reluctantly, and we haven't had cable since. We choose what the kids watch and use DVD time as a treat.

No video games exist in our home. Ethan's in fifth grade and catches a lot of flak for not gaming. One night we talked it over at bedtime. "Mom, my friends say they feel sorry for me, but I feel sorry for them. They don't read, or play the piano, or know martial arts. They just know how to play video games." I don't include that to pat myself on the back. I share it to give you courage. It's okay to raise children who live differently from their peers. After all, the norm of kids addicted to screens is not helping our culture one bit. Here are some other ideas to consider for your plan.

The Priority List. Dannah Gresh realized when her kids transitioned to middle school that she would lose a lot of control over what they were watching. They needed to be able to self-moderate. She had her kids write down their priorities. Their lists included family, time with God, homework, soccer, piano, video games, and time with friends. Then she had her kids put their priorities in order of importance, which made them realize why they didn't get to play video games until homework was done or chores were complete. Dannah says, "Teaching consequential thinking skills was important so they could carry those limits into high school, college, and beyond. Otherwise you're just setting rules."[25]

Nighttime Round Up. Hannah Keeley collects all phones, tablets, and laptops around 10:00 p.m.—even with three college kids living at home. If any of her college kids need to work later on homework, they can ask her for that extra time. "We know what they are doing online because we keep the computers out where we can see them. Every night we have a time when we shut down and a place where all the electronics go."[26]

Track the Time. Kristen Welch observed that so many parents are unaware of how much their children are consuming on screens. She began by watching her children closely and then setting a time limit: thirty minutes on weekdays (kids pick the screen). They use a screen-time chart to keep track. Sometimes they bend the rules to watch family movies, but generally during the week the house rule is thirty minutes a day. In the summers with more free time, the kids can earn screen time by reading.

Media-Free Days. Another thing Kristen did was to have a screen-free day on Sunday. She didn't think it would be a big deal since the kids were already used to restricted media. But when she announced it, there was weeping and gnashing of teeth! The reaction shocked Kristen. She told her kids, "Look at your reaction. This is too important to you. This is why we need to do it." It took weeks of being consistent, but now they never ask to use a screen on Sunday.[27]

Use a Timer. Jennifer Degler employs a screen-time manager—a handy TV Timer BOB—to avoid screen-time battles. She programs thirty minutes on each device, and after that, the device just shuts off. If her children need more time on the computer, she can program that. Her teenage son said, "I just hate that TV timer; you are so controlling. I hope those are still around when I'm a parent because I'm going to use them on my kids."[28]

Screen Time and the Single Mom

How can you reduce your child's screen time and still get the "me" time you so desperately need? One of the best things is to set an early bedtime for your children, particularly for younger kids. When you consistently put your child to bed early, he or she learns to adjust to that routine. If your child isn't ready to fall asleep, you can say, "You don't have to go to sleep right away, but you have to go to your room and be quiet. You can read for a few minutes." This allows the single mom some time at the end of the day to be alone without interruptions.

Your Digital Model

We can't pass on a healthy relationship with technology to our child if we are constantly scrolling through social media, texting during mealtimes, and watching TV in the background. What we model digitally is more important than what we say about screen time. If we as moms are consumed all our waking hours with electronic media of any kind, we are communicating, "This is what life is about. This is the norm." Too often we tell our kids to limit screen time, but then we spend hours online. One day I woke up early to write, but instead of getting ahead, I watched a viral sensation on YouTube. It's so easy to be distracted.

In this digital age, we must be vigilant about our screen time to make sure it doesn't eclipse our parenting time. According to technology addiction therapist Dr. David Greenfield, about 65 percent of people in America abuse technology. He says, "The phone's never off, so we're never off. You sleep with it next to your pillow. We're not designed to be vigilant 24-7."[29]

No wonder we don't have enough energy, patience, or margin to parent. Most moms automatically check their devices several times an hour. Staring at screens is anything but relaxing. It's a good idea to have a screen curfew not only for your kids but for you. How much television are *you* going to watch per day? How long are *you* going to stay online? When you power down all of your devices at the same time each night, it will prepare you to have a better night's rest.

Way before social media, a sixteenth-century French author named François de La Rochefoucauld said, "We are more interested in making others believe we are happy than in trying to be happy ourselves."[30] Stop putting your energy toward projecting a happy life to hundreds of friends online. Just work on the circle in your home. Spend less time online and more time face-to-face, eyeball-to-eyeball with your kids. That's the digital road less traveled toward happiness as a mom.[31]

Today's Energy Boost

Take time to evaluate—honestly evaluate: How much screen time does your child get per day? How much do you?

Today's Prayer

Lord, help me not to allow constant distractions into my life. I don't want to be a slave to my phone or social media. I will not be addicted to texts or tweets. I want to be fully present for my children. Give me wisdom to implement a positive game plan for screens in my home. Help my kids and my spouse to cooperate with screen-time limits in our home.

Day 14

Hit Reset

Create in me a pure heart, O God,
and renew a steadfast spirit within me.

Psalm 51:10

In California it's against the law to drive and talk on your cell phone without a hands-free device. But as James was driving the five of us in our minivan down the freeway, he was jabbering away, phone to his ear. A motorcycle cop pulled up right next to us. He stared at James. Eyeball-to-eyeball at seventy miles per hour. James couldn't have been more busted.

It was eerie, funny, and depressing all at once. We knew this very close encounter with the law was going to cost some money. James pulled over, and our kids stared with wonder at the tall officer coming our way.

"You know you were using a cell phone," the officer said matter-of-factly.

"Yes, officer. I was using my cell phone and I didn't have my headset. I am very sorry," James said.

"Thank you for being honest. Not many people are honest these days. Your honesty is going to get you off."

James and I always joke about the time years ago when he was pulled over on a quiet country road in Virginia for speeding, and the officer's name was, no joke, Officer Justice. And he did mete out justice that day. But on this day, we met *Officer Mercy!*

Since that encounter with Officer Mercy, James has used his headset. Sometimes we need the arm of the law, or something equally jarring, to get us back on the right track.

Take Inventory

The active duty phase of mommyhood is such a busy time that we can forget to take stock of what we're doing right and what we're doing wrong. There's no such thing as the mommy police to write us up a ticket when we lose our way. Who has time for reflection in this nonstop digital age? Life is go-go-go. Yet taking inventory of our home life can help us spot problems before they get big. We need to utilize the reset button and make the most of fresh starts. Dannah Gresh says,

> We'll go crazy if we don't reset. Motherhood is a period like nothing else in your life. There's never a natural reset time. There's never really downtime for you to take inventory and say, how am I doing? Taking the time to do that can give your spirit an "Atta girl…this week went all right."
>
> I remember reading a book about prayer by Fern Nichols. I was confronted about how I handled something with my kids. I knew I had to go back and fix that. It was a reset moment. That prayer time or accountability coffee with a friend gives you that time to go back and say "I didn't do that so well." I'm big on telling my kids I'm sorry. If we don't take time to reset in prayer or in accountability to another person, life's too busy and you never do.[32]

Make the commitment to regularly and honestly review your performance as a mom. This could mean meeting with another friend every week to pray for each other. Or maybe your bedtime ritual will be to review in your mind: *What went right today? What went wrong? Is there anything I wish I would have done differently?* Don't get caught in the trap of striving for perfection, but neither should you fall prey to a life of mediocrity.

Kathi Lipp found some friends to help her reset her attitude about her adult children:

> I had always been a part of a MOPS group or a Moms in Prayer group when my kids were younger. Yet with my adult kids, I found I still needed to be honest with a couple of my friends. It started off as three of us—other authors who seemed to have kids who turned out perfectly. But as we said "things aren't going so

well over here," we realized we were in the same boat. We started a group called the Bad Moms Club. When we're going through a situation, we encourage each other and pray. We remind each other about the great things about our kids and that they probably won't join a cult.[33]

Take time to encourage another mom to good works, to give her a hug when she's down, and to be an honest sounding board. If an accountability partner confronts you with something you need to change, don't make excuses. When you humble yourself and press *reset* in your life, God will lift you up.

A Word for Single Moms from Janet Thompson

Find yourself a godly Christian woman who you admire and who you want to learn from. Look for someone you want praying for you and giving you wisdom when you're going through hard times. You're not looking for a mother or a grandmother for your children, but someone just to be there to support and guide you. Find Christian families who will have you and your kids over so your kids can experience what a godly family looks like. Don't shy away and think, *Now that I'm single, I don't have anything to do with couples and families.* Whatever stage of life you're in, ask yourself: Who's mentoring me and who can I be mentoring? Use the things that are happening to you as a mom to help someone else who is experiencing something similar.[34]

Hi Me, How's It Going?

Here are a few questions you can ask yourself regularly.

How's my delivery? Are you communicating to your kids in a way that's connecting with them? Is your tone usually harsh, sarcastic, wimpy, loving, gentle, happy, or stressed? Get familiar with Gary Chapman's book *The Five Love Languages* and learn how to speak in your child's primary love language. The five love languages are physical touch, words of affirmation, acts of service, gifts, and quality time.[35]

Am I encouraging obedience? You don't want to exasperate your child by being inconsistent with discipline. One day he gets off without any consequences. The next day he gets grounded for a week for the same infraction. He'll grow up with a disdain for authority and that will translate into problems with his walk with God. Your child is learning the habit of obedience or disobedience primarily in your home.

Do I have more than just good intentions? We can substitute having good intentions and knowledge for action. For instance, we buy a book about losing weight and have good intentions about eating healthier and exercising. But until we actually *do* something, our good intentions don't amount to much. We tend to judge ourselves by our good intentions but others by their behavior. Be a mom of action. Good intentions are not enough.

Am I giving my kids enough Vitamin No? You need to establish appropriate boundaries or else you will run yourself ragged and your kids will run wild. *No* is not a dirty word that will squash your child's spirit. It's a beautiful word that allows your child to learn character ("No, you can't watch that"), safety ("No, you can't ride your bike without a helmet"), wisdom ("No, you can't join the team because our schedule is already full"), and respect ("No, because I said so").

Am I smiling or scowling? If my child were to describe me, would he or she picture me smiling or scowling? Make the conscious decision to smile when you greet your child in the morning, when you pick them up from school, when they tell you about their day, at mealtime, and at bedtime. Even if you don't feel like it, give your kids the courtesy, comfort, and brightness of your smile.

You Hold the Key

Once a week, I sweat at an indoor cycling class run out of a trainer's garage in my neighborhood. One morning I walked back home, and the garage door into my house was locked. I didn't have the key. I didn't have my phone. Lucy was with me, riding her bike with training wheels. And I was having my period.

I was so mad at James for locking that door. What an inconvenience! We began walking to my parents' house, which is about ten minutes away...uphill. As I huffed and pushed Lucy's bike up to Grandma's house, the Holy Spirit nudged me, and I had this conversation in my mind: *Why should you be mad at James? He didn't lock the door to keep you out. He thought you had the key. Next time remember your keys!*

I could have called James (when I finally got home and had my phone) to unload my grief on him. But I realized my inconvenient situation was squarely my fault.

You know what, moms? When we stop blaming others or circumstances for our trouble and simply own our stuff, it frees us up to do something about it. Take responsibility for your own actions and hit the reset button when necessary. You hold the key to positive change. Face your mom fears with faith and act as if the answers are on the way.

Today's Energy Boost

How are you going to take inventory of your mommy life? A coffee date with a friend or questions you ask yourself at the end of the day? The reset button is always there, so go forward in hope and use it!

Today's Prayer

Lord, You are a powerful and merciful God who can take my mommy mistakes and missteps and use them for good. Shape my character so I can be the mom You want me to be. Forgive my sins and help me to recognize immediately when I have to make things right with You and with my kids. Thank You that I can start with a clean slate today.

Key 3

HEALTHY

ACTION-ORIENTED

Becoming PRAYERFUL

P

Y

Day 15

God, Not Google

I lift up my eyes to the mountains—
where does my help come from?
My help comes from the LORD,
the Maker of heaven and earth.

PSALM 121:1-2

My friend's son had a growth on his leg. Concerned, she had taken him to the doctor for an exam. She gave me the medical term for it, which sounded like gibberish to me. When I got home, I sat down at my computer to look up the medical term and learn more about it.

When we're faced with a problem, we often turn to Google for the answer. If your child has a cough that just won't stop, you look up medical answers online. If you're overwhelmed by stress, you search for "dealing with stress" and read articles from health organizations and popular magazines about stress management. While there's nothing wrong with seeking information online, there is something terribly wrong when we turn to Google before we turn to God.

The verse at the top of today's reading isn't "I lift up my eyes to my smartphone—where does my help come from? My help comes from Google, the holder of all information." In this digital age, we can get our wires crossed. The answers to your family's problems aren't found on homepages or search engines. The answers you need are found in the ancient pages of God's Word and by speaking to the source of wisdom Himself.

Where Wisdom Resides

James has all sorts of funny ways to answer the telephone, mostly manufactured to discourage telemarketing calls. One of his familiar greetings is, "You got the questions? We got the answers!" That usually causes unwanted callers to hang up abruptly. But the only person who can really use this greeting honestly is God. To use a word picture, when God picks up the phone in response to your call, you can picture Him answering enthusiastically, "You've got the questions? I have the answers!"

One mom I know has a sign on her front door that reads, "Good morning, this is God. I will be handling all your problems today." I like that. The happy mom knows her battles belong to the Lord and that her lifeline is prayer. When the happy mom needs wisdom, she turns to God in prayer and to His Word first. Google comes second (or third or fourth).

James 1:5 says, "If any of you lacks wisdom, you should ask God, who gives generously to all without finding fault, and it will be given to you." In other words, when your toddler is screaming or your teenager is rebelling, ask God for wisdom. Have a conversation with your heavenly Father, and He will give you wisdom for your home life. Here are a few verses about the value of wisdom:

> For wisdom is more precious than rubies,
>   and nothing you desire can compare with her.
>
> (Proverbs 8:11)

> The one who gets wisdom loves life;
>   the one who cherishes understanding will soon prosper.
>
> (Proverbs 19:8)

> Wisdom will save you from the ways of wicked men,
>   from men whose words are perverse.
>
> (Proverbs 2:12)

> Do not forsake wisdom, and she will protect you;
>   love her, and she will watch over you.
>
> (Proverbs 4:6)

> By wisdom a house is built,
>   and through understanding it is established.
>
> (Proverbs 24:3)

> The fear of the LORD is the beginning of knowledge,
>   but fools despise wisdom and instruction.
>
> (Proverbs 1:7)

Kathi Lipp encourages us to have certain verses that speak to us and to go back to them over and over again. She says,

> Prayer does not change God, but it changes me in big ways. It helps me accept the unacceptable. It helps me love my kids when they are unlovable. It helps me trust God when all the circumstances are untrustworthy.[1]

When you need help understanding your life, when you need patience for that child who gets under your skin, it's time to pray. Don't turn to the advice column or psychologist first. Ask *God* for a dose of wisdom. Scripture tells us again and again that the fear of the Lord is the beginning of wisdom. That fear doesn't mean we're scared to talk to God, as if He were waiting with a lightning bolt to zap us. The fear of the Lord is a deep awe and respect for His name. It's the awareness we are in the presence of a holy and just God who holds us accountable for our thoughts and deeds. That He is God, and we are not. When we fear the Lord, wisdom is a beautiful byproduct.

Data Dependency

This little dandy is probably in your purse or pocket. It's only a few inches wide and probably never more than a few feet away from you. Yes, it's your phone. One study found that on average, people use their mobile devices 150 times a day.[2] A global study by Cisco Systems suggests that nine of ten people under the age of thirty suffer from "nomophobia," which is the fear of being disconnected from our gadgets.[3] We rely on the data on our phones for decision making. We check the weather, traffic, and school updates at our fingertips. We have more confidence and more control—and seemingly less need of God.

Think about it. Could you go a whole day without talking to God? Probably. Could you go a whole day without your cell phone or any Internet access? Ouch, that would hurt more, wouldn't it? We are ever dependent on our calorie trackers, social media posts, playlists, texts, and emails. Instead of nurturing a dependency on the Divine, we've nurtured a dependency on data. We talk to God once in a while at our convenience, but we need our phones and devices 24/7.

Living in a digital world as a mom can be frenetic, fast-paced, and overwhelming. Being online constantly throughout the day is not calming. According to the Barna Group, more than seven out of ten adults admit to being overwhelmed by the amount of information they need to stay up to date.[4] We need to pull away from Google and rest in God.

Studies even show that people who spend time close to nature exhibit greater attentiveness and stronger memory. Their brains are calmer and sharper.[5] Remember the words of the psalmist: "I lift my eyes to the *mountains*." You don't have to wait until a vacation to experience the calming effect of nature. You can talk a five-minute prayer walk around your neighborhood or simply look outside the window as you talk to the Creator of it all. There's a richness only silence and stillness offers, but we seldom have the patience to wait on God in our 140-character tweet world.

Today our idols aren't golden calves or wooden images. They're phones and tablets and laptops and DVRs. Of course technology should be used and can be used for good in your mom life. But if you follow the culture's growing dependence on technology, you won't need God nearly as much as you need Wi-Fi.

Starting Over

Do you check your phone first thing in the morning? If so, you're like 40 percent of all adults and 56 percent of millennials.[6] I heard Sheila Walsh share something simple you can do instead. First thing in the morning, she says, "Good morning, Father." When I used this greeting, I realized something beautiful. In the same way I said good morning to my kids and made their breakfast and checked their backpacks, God was looking out for me. My heavenly Father was preparing my day too. As you say "Good morning, Father," you can hear Him saying back to you, "Good morning, my child." Every day you get the chance to start over. Fix your attention on God first before you fixate on your phone.

So how do you become a more prayerful mom? Don't worry—no 4:00 a.m. wakeup call or Bible degree required. You simply start with love for God and an earnest desire to communicate with your heavenly Father. Author Stormie Omartian didn't begin as an expert on prayer. She simply recognized her desperate need for prayer as a mom, and she did something about it. In *The Power of a Praying Parent*, she writes:

> I learned to identify every concern, fear, worry, or possible scenario that came into my mind as a prompting by the Holy Spirit to pray for that particular thing. As I covered [my son] Christopher in prayer and released him into God's hands, God released my mind from that particular concern. This doesn't mean that once I prayed for something I never prayed about it again, but at least for a time I was relieved of the burden. When it surfaced again, I prayed about it again. God didn't promise that nothing bad would ever happen to my child, but praying released the power of God to work in his life, and I could enjoy more peace in the process.[7]

Do you need more peace as a mom? That peace won't be found in googling your questions. It's found in laying your burdens at the feet of the God who cares for you. You are His precious child. He's waiting to talk with you today, and unlike most of us, He's not in a rush.

Today's Energy Boost

Tomorrow when you wake up, begin the day by saying, "Good morning, Father."

Today's Prayer

Lord, indeed my help does come from You, the Maker of heaven and earth. Forgive me for relying on Google for answers. I realize You are the source of wisdom. Teach me how to pray effectively for myself and my family. I leave my concerns at Your feet. Please fill me with Your peace today.

Day 16

Help, I Want to Be a Praying Mom!

Pour out your heart like water
in the presence of the Lord.
Lift up your hands to him
for the lives of your children.

LAMENTATIONS 2:19

If you want to learn how to cook, you can buy an easy recipe book or watch a few cooking shows. Need help with your wardrobe? There are countless style magazines and websites, wardrobe consultants, and bargain designer clothing stores. While cooking yummy meals is certainly a plus, and looking your best is a good thing, there's one mommy skill that's even more important to learn for your family: *prayer*.

I wanted help for my prayer life, so I asked Fern Nichols, the founder of Moms in Prayer, about her own journey as a praying mom. Moms in Prayer is a ministry of moms from more than 140 nations who meet together in small groups to pray for their children and their schools.[8] This international ministry began in the heart of one anxious mom sending off her sons to junior high. Fern realized she needed God now more than ever and that her sons would need a lot of protective prayer. "Lord," she prayed, "there must be one mom who feels the same way who will come to my house and pray with me." God brought a mom friend to Fern's mind and she immediately called her. God had prepared her friend because she quickly replied, "Yes, we must get together and pray!" That's how this international ministry started more than thirty years ago—from two ordinary moms who needed hope and peace as they sent their children off to school.

Matthew 18:19-20 says, "Again, truly I tell you that if two of you on earth agree about anything they ask for, it will be done for them by my Father in heaven. For where two or three gather in my name, there am I with them."

There is power in praying with another mom or a group of moms for your kids. The power is in the agreement and the unity. Maybe you feel intimidated by praying out loud with other moms. What if you don't know what to say? Or even worse, what if you say the wrong thing? What if the other moms are better at praying than you are? Listen to Fern's reassuring words,

> I tell a mom who's afraid of saying the wrong thing, just think of a three- or four-year-old child who's trying to express something to his mommy, and he just doesn't say it right. Yet the mom hears and understands. She wants the child to speak no matter how he may mix up his words. Sincerity of heart—that's what God is looking for. No matter how it is expressed, He understands. What I love about the Holy Spirit is that He takes our muttering and not knowing how to say it, and He says it perfectly to the Lord.

> When Jesus commanded us to pray, He didn't command us to do anything that would harm us ever. He knew prayer would develop a deepening love relationship with Him. And that's what prayer is all about. It is fellowship with the God who has saved us. He wants to love on us and bless us. The greatest benefit of prayer is getting to know God and trusting Him.

Come with Your Needs

I joined a Moms in Prayer group when Ethan was in first grade. He goes to public school and I wanted to cover his little life in prayer. One meeting, I asked the moms to pray that Ethan would find one Christian friend at school. The very next day, Ethan excitedly told me, "Guess what? I found a Christian in my school." A boy was singing "Joy to the World," and Ethan asked if he was a Christian. He said yes. He not only was in Ethan's class, he sat right next to him. God answers prayer.

Fern Nichols has a similar story of answered prayer. Her grandson was about to begin first grade, and he had a bad dream that he couldn't find the lunchroom, which made him worry all the more. Fern's group prayed for him that he wouldn't be fearful on the first day of school and that Jesus would be right there with him. On the first day, Fern received a picture of her grandson at lunch with six friends smiling broadly. God cares about a little boy and his lunch.

As our kids get older, our prayer requests grow more serious. We switch from "Lord, please help my child learn to tie his shoes" to "Lord, protect my child from pornography, drugs, and bad friends." If we as moms aren't praying for our kids, who is? Possibly a praying grandma, but the point still stands: prayer matters and your child needs *you* to ask God to intervene in his or her life every day. Jesus is waiting for you to come to Him with your needs. Fern says,

> We are burdened. We are carrying things that are deeply grievous to us—our finances, home, children, or husband. Hear Jesus's voice saying, "Oh My daughter, come to Me. You're heavy laden, but I want to give you rest. Will you roll that burden on Me? I can handle it. I can take care of it." When He tells us to cast our cares on Him, He's not teasing us.
>
> The more we trust Him on that, the more we can walk in the assurance that God is the blessed controller of all things. We do not need to worry or fret. When we don't pray, we don't know what to do with our troubles. That affects the whole family because if mom isn't happy, nobody's happy. A praying mom gives an atmosphere to the home that's joyful, peaceful, and welcoming. Even in those times when things aren't rosy and the answers have not come, there can still be the deep joy and satisfaction of knowing that God's got it. What we find is that when we come to pray for our kids, God shapes *us* up![9]

Prayer as Easy as 1-2-3-4

Moms in Prayer uses the following four steps in prayer. You can incorporate these into your personal prayer life as well.

Step 1: Praise. Praise God for who He is. Take an attribute of God found in the Bible and pray that back to Him in praise. For instance, you might read Genesis 14:19, which says, "'Blessed be Abram by God Most High, Creator of heaven and earth.'" Then you can pray, *Lord, I praise You because You are the God Most High, the Creator of heaven and earth.*

Step 2: Confession. In a group, you can have a time of silent confession. On your own, you can confess your sins silently or out loud. We know from 1 John 1:9 that if we confess our sins before God, He will forgive us.

Step 3: Thanksgiving. Thank God for answered prayer and for His provision in your family.

Step 4: Intercession. There are over seven thousand promises in God's Word, and you can claim these promises for your kids. Praying the Scriptures is essential and effective. You can take a verse and insert your child's name. For example, using Romans 12:12, *Father, I pray that (your child's name) rejoices in hope, is patient in affliction, and that he/she would be faithful in prayer.*

See, it's not that hard, is it? Since I have prayed using these four steps, my confidence level and peace as a parent has skyrocketed. I know when my kids face something at school, such as a mean friend or a speech contest, that everything is going to turn out all right because I have prayed about it with other moms.

Your heavenly Father is waiting to hear your voice, which is a sweet sound in His ear.

Today's Energy Boost

Visit the Moms in Prayer website at www.MomsinPrayer.org. If you have a child in school, see if there's a group of moms already praying for your school by clicking "Groups" and then "Find a group" on the website.

Today's Prayer

Lord, I want to be a praying mom. Thank You that You hear my prayers. I ask that (insert child's name) will be a peacemaker who plants seeds of peace and reaps a harvest of righteousness (James 3:18). I pray that (insert child's name) would do everything without complaining or arguing, so that they may be innocent and pure as God's perfect children who live in a world of corrupt and sinful people (Philippians 2:14-15).

Praying When Your Kids Are Going Haywire

From one man he made all the nations, that they should inhabit the whole earth; and he marked out their appointed times in history and the boundaries of their lands. God did this so that they would seek him and perhaps reach out from him and find him, though he is not far from any one of us.

Acts 17:26-27

My friend Rhonda Rhea and her husband had five babies in seven years. She jokes that the Lord gathered the angels around Him, pointed to their family, and said, "Guys, watch this! It's going to be real funny!" Like the time Rhonda went out to dinner with her husband, leaving their fourteen-year-old in charge at home. During the date, she received a call from her twelve-year-old.

"Mom, what gets blood out of carpet? Should I use Lemon Pledge or bleach?"

"Put down the chemicals and step away from the carpet," Rhonda said. "What happened?"

They ended up going to the hospital since one of the kids had fallen down the stairs and needed stitches.

Family life is full of the unexpected. When you think everything is going well, the phone rings, the cat wanders into the living room covered in pudding, and your toddler throws up in the toy box (yes, that happened to Rhonda too).[10]

Whether it is behavior issues, messes to clean, destructive choices, or health problems, our kids can go haywire. Haywire is defined as "not functioning properly, disorganized, erratic or crazy."[11] Sound familiar?

You Are Not Alone

When we were brand-new parents, we lovingly referred to our first-born as "the lump." Ethan was like a sack of potatoes, not moving an inch unless we helped him. That lump was seven pounds of pure heaven on earth—well, until he cried and went haywire, which happened to be often.

I remember when he was about six weeks old, and he was crying and crying upstairs in his crib. I had all my parenting books cracked open, sprawled across the kitchen table. Was he hungry? Wet? Needing to be held? Too hot, too cold? I trudged up the stairs, and by the time I reached his bedroom door, he had raised the volume a few decibels. I walked over to his crib and stood over my little screaming lump.

"How are you doing, little one?" I asked.

To my utter surprise, he stopped crying immediately. His chocolate-chip brown eyes connected to mine. His body relaxed and he melted into his sheets. He blinked a few times, then closed his eyes. Slowly and gingerly I backed out of the room, pausing in the hallway to see if the tirade would begin again. It didn't. A few minutes later, I peeked in to find my lump fast asleep.

That was the first time I remember Ethan being soothed simply by my presence. He didn't need to be fed or diapered. He didn't need the heat turned on or off. He didn't even need to be held or touched. He only needed the reassurance that he was not alone.

Kids aren't the only ones who need reassurance. We moms need to know we're not alone—especially when our kids are screaming their heads off.

Kathi Lipp writes in her book *I Need Some Help Here!*,

> One of the most powerful sentences in the English language is "Me too!" It helps us discover who our people are. Some of my closest friends started out as acquaintances who, once their children went off the rails, became my mom army. My closest comrades in arms...
>
> I know that your kids will not always do things the way you would want them to. Your toddler will throw tantrums. Your

preschooler will be defiant. Your preteen will be disrespectful. Your teenager will throw tantrums (yes, sadly, we circle back to that). And mine have too. It's pretty much a motherhood guarantee: your kid will break your heart.

But I have another guarantee for you. Once your heart has been broken for your kids, God can use that brokenness to woo you to be the kind of parent he needs you to be. You just must be willing to hand them over to him. He will do the hard work of restoration for you because you are his child.[12]

When your children aren't turning out according to plan, go straight to the Creator and pray about your kids. Hand them over to God and allow Him to do the work of restoration. The Bible says in Psalm 55:22,

> Cast your cares on the LORD
>   and he will sustain you;
> he will never let
>   the righteous be shaken.

Find other godly moms who can support you through the tough times of parenting. When Karen Ehman was having a rough day, she called her friend Micca Campbell, who passed along one of her grandmother's sayings: "Sometimes you need to stop talking to your kids about God, and start talking to God about your kids." Karen realized:

> Sometimes if all I'm doing is preach, preach, preaching to my kids with my finger pointed, they don't hear me. Sometimes I need to be quiet and go talk to God about my kids. I wear through the knees of my jeans more now than when my kids were younger. When they were little, I was homeschooling and they were always within my sight. Sad to say, that was probably when my prayer life was the worst. Why pray? I had it all handled. Everybody was around the table. But as they grew older, less was in my control.[13]

Have you ever thought the lack of control you're experiencing may actually be a good thing because it drives you to depend on God? As much as we hate to admit it, we are not in charge. I certainly discovered that one ordinary spring day.

In Him We Live

I was sitting at my desk, typing at the computer with two-year-old Lucy babbling next me. *The big kids should be coming home from school any minute*, I thought. They were riding bikes home with James. I had just begun recording Lucy's babbling for a keepsake when the phone rang. It was James. "Ethan got hit by a car. We're close to home. Get Lucy and come." I could hear Ethan crying in the background.

I scooped up Lucy, and I was shaking as we headed for the van. Going down our street and turning the corner, I saw bikes strewn on the side of the road and a few cars backing up. I heard the police sirens coming. A little group was crowding on the sidewalk. I couldn't believe that I was the mom walking onto this scene.

There was my Ethan, lying on the road, crying. He wasn't bleeding and didn't seem seriously injured. I told him not to worry, that God was with him. The paramedics arrived, fitted him with a neck brace, and put him on a stretcher. He was crying softly the whole time.

Things began to move very quickly. James would ride in the ambulance with Ethan. I would follow in the van with Noelle and Lucy.

The police officer wanted to examine Ethan's bike, which was mangled. "When we hear bike versus car," he said, "we just cringe because of what it can mean."

The driver of the car wasn't to blame. Ethan had made a wide right turn, expecting the road to be empty, but it wasn't. When the driver saw Ethan, he immediately stepped on the brake, but not before Ethan plowed into his front bumper. Maybe if that driver had been going five mph faster or if he hadn't slammed on his brake, I would be writing a different story. Certainly the story would have been different had Ethan not been wearing a helmet.

I knew there would be a lot of paperwork and waiting at the hospital, so I made a little detour on the way to buy Ethan a LEGO set. Can you picture me standing in line while my son was on his way to the hospital in an ambulance? It sounds like a ludicrous use of time, but I wanted to create a memory for him that when bad things happen, God can make something good come out of them (like getting a new LEGO set).

What a surprise to arrive at the hospital, gift in hand, and see a smiling Ethan shuffling around the room like a senior citizen trapped in a seven-year-old body. He giggled about his ambulance ride and how he couldn't see anything because he was staring at the ceiling the whole time. He was wearing new sweat pants from the hospital that ended up costing a small fortune (not to mention the ambulance ride). But other than bruises, there was nothing wrong with him. No broken bones. No brain injuries. No internal bleeding.

I cannot express the relief I felt when Ethan was tucked in his own bed that night, healthy and whole. For the first time, I felt the weight of the verse in Acts 17:28, "For in him we live and move and have our being." Ethan's life could have ended or been severely altered that day. As moms, we cannot control everything in our child's life. That control is reserved only for a Sovereign God. It's *in Him* that our kids live and move and have their being.

Our job as moms is to make sure our kids put their bike helmets on. Beyond that, anything can happen. That's why we pray to a God who sees. Every breath we draw is by the grace of God. He's in control, even when our kids are going haywire.

A Word for Stepmoms from Laura Petherbridge

Since I had two stepmoms growing up, I thought I would know how to be a stepmom myself. That was naïve and erroneous thinking! I learned within the first year as a young Christian, if this blended family was going to survive and no one was going to end up dead or injured—or if I wasn't going to end up in an orange jumpsuit— I needed to really start praying, *Lord, help me see these children through Your eyes. Help me to see them through their pain rather than through my pain. Help me remember what it was like to be a child of divorce. Use that childhood pain in my own life for Your glory Lord, so I can be a godly influence to these hurting boys.*

Prayer was my lifeline. I prayed that I would respond as Christ would respond even when I was hurt, angry, or rejected. In time, my prayers morphed into thanksgiving. *Thank You that the one gift I can give these two young men is the example of what a healthy, stable marriage looks like. Let me be an illustration of how a woman should treat her husband, so they'll see that and desire that in their own marriages.*[14]

Today's Energy Boost

Take the burden of your child's bad choices off your shoulders and place them on God's. You cannot live your child's life. But you can pray that he or she will obey the Word of God and live.

Today's Prayer

Lord, You have a plan for my child. You are in control. When he or she doesn't do what I want, give me wisdom as a mom. Give me patience when I want to react in anger. Show me what my child looks like through Your eyes. I trust You to work all things together for good in my child's life.

Making the Most of Popcorn Prayers

LORD my God, give attention to your servant's prayer
and his plea for mercy. Hear the cry and the prayer
that your servant is praying in your presence.

2 CHRONICLES 6:19

It was Sunday morning and my kids were home sick. Feeling especially creative, I grabbed a Bible story about Noah, pictures of animals to color, stuffed animals, and a music CD. I told the kids I needed forty minutes to shower and get ready. Ethan, who was about five, was obsessed with our new timer cube that could be flipped to countdown five, fifteen, thirty, or sixty minutes. Since there wasn't a designation for forty minutes, he decided to set it to five minutes and flip it over and over again.

Beep, beep! Beep, beep! I wanted to throw it out the window after the fourth time it went off. "Ethan, stop using that timer!" I yelled out of my bathroom. Instead of taking a relaxing shower, I was getting all worked up. Negative thoughts flooded my mind. *My kids are driving me crazy. What are we going to do all cooped up, sick on this rainy day? I'm so tired.* I shot a prayer heavenward. "Lord, help me. I don't feel like teaching the Bible anymore. I'm sorry—I am not being patient with my kids." I wondered how I had clicked from Sunday school teacher to sinner so fast.

But after that short, yet sincere, prayer, a sense of peace and calm filled me. My attitude toward the kids (and that loud timer) changed. We did have home church about Noah, complete with coloring and music and skits, and it was actually fun. I remember thinking, *Wow, sentence prayers work!*

Shoot Them Up

When your children are young, it may be unrealistic to imagine yourself sitting in a quiet room with the sunlight seeping in as you sip your coffee and write in your prayer journal. Karen Ehman remembers she used to beat herself up about this. She had an infant, a toddler, and was homeschooling a first grader. She didn't have the whitespace in her day like her friends who had kids in public or private school. Karen recalls,

> I had to get my eyes off that other mom because I would be jealous when they would say, "Oh, the school bus just pulled away and I poured myself a cup of coffee to do my Bible study. I spent an hour and a half on the lesson." I would be like, "Are you kidding me? I pray between bites and sips and gulps and wipes."
>
> I had to get creative and see where I could mother and spiritually multitask at the same time. I used to go to a fast-food restaurant and let my kids play in the ball pit for a good hour. I would take my Bible and have my quiet time right in the middle of that noisy restaurant. Or I would put Bible verses on index cards and stick them in the minivan. I had to do what I wished was an hour-long morning quiet time in little snippets of six or seven mini-sessions throughout the day.
>
> I had to learn that it wasn't possible for me to have this picture-perfect, cup-of-coffee, Instagram-worthy quiet time with God. There's never a time to put our spiritual life on hold. We just have to be creative and be flexible.[15]

Throughout the day, you can breathe sentence prayers and shoot them up to heaven. After a bedtime prayer with Noelle when she was five, she told me she prays all day long.

"That's good, Noelle," I said. "When do you pray?"

"At school, in the bathroom, walking around. Sometimes I whisper."

"What do you say?" I asked.

"Jesus, I love You. You are the best person ever. I worship You. I will worship You all my life."

Wow, the lessons we can learn from our kids! If only I could remember to say those things throughout the day to Jesus. Fern Nichols has this advice about praising God:

A mom with little ones around her feet can get up ten minutes early and meditate on an attribute of who her God is. If you don't get through your requests, don't worry. All day long, you can be shooting up requests for help. But what's really sweet about that beginning time is you can start your day knowing God is with you in that attribute. When you focus on an attribute of God, it will give you stability throughout the day because your mind will be on the God who you have just praised.[16]

Here are a couple of attributes of God to get you started:

God is omnipotent—He is all powerful, possessing unlimited power or authority.

> For who in the skies above can compare with the LORD?
> Who is like the LORD among the heavenly beings?
> In the council of the holy ones God is greatly feared;
> he is more awesome than all who surround him.
> (Psalm 89:6-7)

God is faithful—He is constant, loyal, reliable, steadfast, unwavering, devoted, true, dependable.

> Know therefore that the LORD your God is God; he is the faithful God, keeping his covenant of love to a thousand generations of those who love him and keep his commandments (Deuteronomy 7:9).

The more biblical your prayer life becomes the more effective and meaningful it will be. One thing I love about being in a Moms in Prayer group is that each week we pray Bible verses for our children. I know there's power in our prayer. Being part of a weekly prayer group puts prayer on my calendar and that ensures it gets done. I can live on popcorn prayers, but it's good to have a meal with friends once a week in more focused prayer for our children.

Dannah Gresh reminds us that every mom is different. For her, she needs a lot of organization to feel like she's being proactive. She writes Scriptures on sticky notes and puts them on her bathroom mirror to remind her to pray those verses for her kids.[17] But some moms might feel that writing a sticky note is too rigid. They are more free-spirited and prefer to simply pray out loud as they feel led.

Don't get caught up in formulas and dos and don'ts. Simply make time in your everyday life to talk to God, read His Word, and pray for your kids. You might listen to the Bible while you work out or pray as you walk. You might pray for each child by name as you fold his or her laundry. You might pray for your family while you're standing at the kitchen sink. Make the most of your in-between moments to talk with God and also put time in your schedule for prayer.

When You're in a Hole, Pray

It was a sunny San Diego afternoon and we were walking at Sunset Cliffs along the coast. James and Noelle went down a more challenging path, while Ethan, Lucy (at eighteen months), and I headed toward an easier way. The dirt path dipped down two feet into a large hole that you had to walk through before stepping back up onto the trail. I thought I had it all under control. But when I set my foot down, my ankle twisted, and I hurled forward into that hole, clutching Lucy for dear life. The angels must have surrounded her because she didn't have a scratch or bruise on her from that fall. I absorbed the impact with my shoulder. My hands were all scratched up. And I couldn't move my right ankle.

Ethan, who was six, looked petrified. Even though I was petrified too, I said, "I'm fine. I just hurt my ankle. We're going to be okay. Just yell for help." He started yelling at the top of his lungs, "Help! Help!" In between his yells, I yelled "James!" and Lucy yelled "Daddy!" But no one heard us and no one came.

I prayed, "Lord, send someone to get me out of this hole." It was the first time I remember feeling totally helpless as a mom. I was lying on my back holding on to Lucy, unable to get up on my own. We were vulnerable, alone on a trail. We were counting on God. A few minutes went by, and then a woman heard Ethan's cries for help and found us. She picked up Lucy out of the hole, and then she began to pull me out.

"Come help, Ethan," she said, and I thought, *Wow, how does she know Ethan's name?* But it was her Ethan, a junior high boy who came into the picture and lifted me to my feet.

Five minutes later, James and Noelle came into view. We yelled and waved our arms frantically like the passengers stranded on Gilligan's Island. We got to urgent care, and thankfully my foot wasn't broken, just sprained. I wrote some lessons in my journal after that leisure day gone wrong:

- Stay together in your family. Don't split up. There's strength in staying together.

- When you're in a hole, remain calm. Pray and ask for God's help. He will send it—maybe in unusual ways.

- Be patient with the process.

Maybe you're in a crisis time in your family. When you find yourself in a hole, pray. Scream at the top of your lungs, "Daddy!" God will hear your prayer and come right away. He hears your popcorn prayers. Each one is important to Him.

Today's Energy Boost

Think about your daily routine. Where are some places you can fit in popcorn prayers? During your commute or meal prep time? First thing in the morning for ten minutes?

Today's Prayer

Lord, You are a faithful and powerful God. Thank You for hearing my prayers whether they are short or long. As it says in Psalm 141:2, "May my prayer be set before you like incense; may the lifting up of my hands be like the evening sacrifice."

Day 19

To Infinity and Beyond

*I pray that the eyes of your heart may be enlightened in
order that you may know the hope to which he has called
you, the riches of his glorious inheritance in his holy people,
and his incomparably great power for us who believe.*

Ephesians 1:18-19

I was sitting at breakfast with the kids. I had just read Jonah 3:3, which
says, "Jonah obeyed the word of the Lord and went to Nineveh." Feeling like a very good mom about to impart a wise spiritual lesson, I asked,
"Wouldn't it have been better for Jonah to obey the Lord right away instead
of being thrown overboard and swallowed by a large fish? He could have
missed all that pain and terror simply by saying yes to God in the first
place."

To my surprise, Ethan said, "I'd rather go through all the trouble. That
way you know for sure you *have* to do what God says. What God asked
Jonah to do was hard. I'd want to make sure it was really God who was
asking me to go to Nineveh."

How funny yet true. Sometimes we have to learn the hard way to
obey the Lord...and so do our kids. God's story for each of us is different. In another breakfast conversation, probably after watching *Aladdin*,
Ethan said, "Wouldn't it be nice to have a genie? I would know the future.
I could get ready in zero seconds. I could get a million tickets for the store
at church."

I laughed. "Yes, and I'd use my genie to keep you all in bed longer!"

"But then if we had a genie," Ethan mused, "we'd miss the story."

Wisdom from the mouths of babes. If God acted as a magic genie in your life, you'd miss the adventure of His glorious unfolding, as Steven Curtis Chapman sings about in his song "The Glorious Unfolding." Your prayers for your children, from when they are babies to when they have a full head of gray, will be used to unfold a magnificent story only God can write. You have someone better than a genie on your side. You might even say you have a spy.

The Spy on Your Side

After her teen daughter got her first smartphone, a friend of mine felt prompted by the Holy Spirit to check it. When she picked up the phone, she was shocked to see a text from a boy inviting her daughter to have sex with him. Because this mom intercepted that text and had a heart-to-heart talk with her daughter (after getting on her face before God in prayer), that girl remained pure. The Holy Spirit intervened in that family in a specific way to save that daughter from sin and death.

If you are listening, the Holy Spirit will let you know when something is wrong with your children. He will give you the words to say when you're not sure how to respond. Karol Ladd remembers the ups and downs of junior high for her girls. One day someone is your friend and the next day, you're her enemy. Karol says,

> When you pick them up from school and they're crying because so-and-so ditched them at lunch, there's an opportunity to whisper a prayer. *Lord, give me wisdom about what to say now.* Sometimes we just have to listen. Sometimes there's a good word to say. Sometimes they might just need a hug.

One of Karol's daughters was going through a rough time in college. As Karol drove to meet her, she prayed the Lord would give her exactly the right words to say. She knew in her heart and mind the Lord was telling her just to hug her. But that wasn't the answer Karol was looking for.

> I thought, *Lord, no no*! I have so many good words for her. Yet I continued to feel impressed: just hug her. So I said, *Okay, Lord, I'm going to trust You. I've been asking for wisdom and I'm going to trust this is what You're telling me to do here.* So when I greeted her, I just hugged her. She just fell apart in my arms. She cried and

cried. The only thing she could say was, "Mom, this is exactly what I needed. I didn't need to hear your words. I just needed to feel your hug."

I thought, *O Lord, thank You.* He gave me what I needed—His wisdom from above. My wisdom wasn't so great. God's wisdom goes much farther than what I could ask or imagine.[18]

John 14:26 says, "But the Advocate, the Holy Spirit, whom the Father will send in my name, will teach you all things and will remind you of everything I have said to you." You have the Holy Spirit on your side to help you as a mom. You're not the only one watching out for your child.

Make Him a Daniel

When Pam Farrel was pregnant with her first child, Brock, she prayed, *God, give him the faith of a Daniel. Give him the courage to stand for You— even the courage to stand alone for You. Make him a strong witness of light in this dark world. God, may many come to know You because of the life of this little one.*

In high school, Pam saw the answer to that prayer in very obvious ways. Active in his faith, Brock hosted parties where he shared about Christ. As a result, thirty-four of his friends made decisions for Christ by the end of his freshmen year. Brock helped launch a Fellowship of Christian Athletes (FCA) club at school to help these friends grow in their faith. At FCA camp, Brock was challenged to think of ways to be more outspoken on campus. He remembered hearing reports that the Supreme Court had restricted football players from saying a prayer before a game in Texas. He decided to take a stand. Pam writes in *The 10 Best Decisions Every Parent Can Make,*

> Brock called up his buddies on the team and said, "This week, after we beat Fallbrook, I'm going to the 50-yard line to pray. Will you join me? I'm going to call all the guys and the other teams' FCA huddle. So, win or lose, can I count on you to be at the 50?" They all said, "You bet. We're there for ya, man!"
>
> At the Moms in Prayer group that morning, I shared Brock's plan with the moms, and we prayed for all the guys, just as we'd prayed for them before every team outreach.

That opponent was expected to be the hardest they would meet all season, and they were. Brock's team lost 38-0. After the game, the team was discouraged, disappointed, and disillusioned. With heads down, the team wandered aimlessly to their locker room, but Brock went straight to the 50-yard line. He knelt down—all alone.

Pam's heart as a mom ached to see her boy all alone on that football field. She asked her husband Bill if she should join him, but he wisely said, "A varsity quarterback does not want his mom to come on the field to help him with anything! He'll be all right."

Soon, three other players from the opposing team joined Brock at the 50 to pray. Pam headed towards the field with Bill and Brock's younger brothers. She held his face in her hands and said,

> "I have never been more proud of you than I am in this moment. I know tonight was one of the hardest nights of your life. I know you are disappointed at the loss and that your team didn't join you at the 50. But you kept your word to God. Those who honor God, God honors. Brock, I don't know how and I don't know when, but God will honor you for this."[19]

It didn't take God very long. At the next game just one week later, there were forty guys praying at the 50.

Some days your kids will stand alone on their convictions. Other days they will stand leading an army. Our job as moms is not to shield them from disappointment or arrange perfect outcomes. Our job is to pray. Prayer to a faithful God supercharges your parenting, gives you peace, and accomplishes what you cannot. You can be confident knowing that God's got your child...to infinity and beyond.

Today's Energy Boost

Picture your child standing alone someday for their faith and values. Instead of feeling nervous or scared for your child, imagine Almighty God walking alongside your child. Your child is fully protected and never alone.

Today's Prayer

Thank You, Holy Spirit, for being my Advocate. May my son be like Daniel—ever true to his God and courageous, willing to stand alone. May my daughter be like Esther—humble and strong, used by You for such a time as this. May my child know the hope of Your calling, the riches of Your inheritance, and Your great power in their life.

Key 4

HEALTHY

ACTION-ORIENTED

PRAYERFUL

Becoming PERSEVERANT

Y

Leave Me Alone, I'm Hiding in the Bathroom

When the angel of the LORD appeared to Gideon, he
said, "The LORD is with you, mighty warrior."

JUDGES 6:12

As a mom, sometimes your only place of solace is the tiniest room of your home—the bathroom. Hunkered down on the toilet, you hope no one will find you. When Ethan was two, he loved to turn off the light when I was using the bathroom and shut the door. There I was, sitting in the darkness with a toddler snickering on the other side of the door. I didn't reprimand him. I just sat there, content in the dark because at least I was *alone*.

There are moments in motherhood when you'd like to play hide and seek...and be found a few days later. Kathi Lipp talks about her friend who put a playpen in the living room, not for her children but for her. Since the kids crawled on her all day long, she put herself in the playpen where they couldn't touch her![1]

Believe it or not, we can find comfort from a reluctant warrior named Gideon who was hiding out too. He was threshing wheat in a winepress instead of out in the open. He was hiding it from his enemies, the Midianites. Here's the background from Judges 6:1-6 (MSG):

> God put them under the domination of Midian for seven years. Midian overpowered Israel. Because of Midian, the People of Israel made for themselves hideouts in the mountains—caves

and forts. When Israel planted its crops, Midian and Amalek, the easterners, would invade them, camp in their fields, and destroy their crops all the way down to Gaza. They left nothing for them to live on, neither sheep nor ox nor donkey. Bringing their cattle and tents, they came in and took over, like an invasion of locusts. And their camels—past counting! They marched in and devastated the country. The People of Israel, reduced to grinding poverty by Midian, cried out to GOD for help.

If this passage were rewritten for moms today, perhaps it might read like this:

God put them under the domination of needy babies and tantrum-throwing toddlers. The crying children overpowered the mothers. Because of their whiny, unhappy, willful little ones, the mothers made themselves hideouts wherever they could find them—the bathroom, local Starbucks, or locked up in the laundry room. When the moms tried to make food, the kids would wreak havoc in the kitchen and family room. They took over like an invasion of locusts! And their toys multiplied—past counting! They devastated the once Martha Stewart like home. The mothers, reduced to wearing sweats and putting food in little Baggies all day, cried out to God for help.

The Lord Is With You, Mighty Warrior Mom

Right in the middle of Gideon's work, as he was sweating and threshing wheat, the angel of the Lord appears to him and says, "The LORD is with you, mighty warrior." No doubt, Gideon looked behind him for a superhero in the shadows because surely *he* was not that warrior.

Dale Carnegie shares this principle in his book *How to Win Friends and Influence People*: "Give the other person a fine reputation to live up to. If you want to improve a person in a certain respect, act as though that particular trait were already one of his or her outstanding characteristics."[2]

See what the Lord did for Gideon? He gave him a fine reputation to live up to—God saw him as a mighty warrior. Imagine yourself separating darks from whites in the laundry room or going down the grocery aisle when the Lord Jesus appears to you saying, "The Lord is with you, mighty warrior mom." It would change your life to hear those words.

So hear this today: if God is for you, who can be against you? Begin to see yourself as the warrior God has designed you to be to protect and guide your children. Act as if you are a strong mom who's a force to be reckoned with, not because of your strength but because of God's power working through you. Gideon goes on to ask, "If the LORD is with us, why has all this happened to us? Now the LORD has abandoned us and given us into the hand of Midian." You may feel like you are a mom who has been abandoned by God, especially by the end of a long day.

When Ethan was about two, we lost him on purpose in Walmart. Like most young kids, he would always stop and look at toy trains or cars. We were constantly waiting for him and prodding him to catch up. Well, one day we turned the tables. While he stopped to look at Thomas the Train bedding, I kept on walking ahead with the cart. James ducked in the next aisle. When Ethan looked up from his beloved Thomas a minute later, he realized we were gone. Tears filled his eyes and he started to wail. A nice mom started toward him, but James caught her eye and shooed her away.

About thirty seconds later, James scooped up Ethan and said, "When you're in a store, you have to follow me, okay? There are a lot of people in here and we don't want you to get lost. I was watching you the whole time, but I wanted to make sure you understood that you have to follow me or else you'll get lost." Ethan got the message loud and clear.

When we feel abandoned by God, it would be good to remember Ethan crying in Walmart. James didn't abandon Ethan; he was watching him the whole time. It was Ethan who got distracted and took his eyes off his father. We can get distracted by a million little things and take our eyes off Jesus. No wonder we feel abandoned and alone. But when we call out to our heavenly Father, He scoops us up and says, "Don't worry, I've been here the whole time. You just got a little lost. You have to follow Me, okay?"

I think many times we have it backward. We say to Jesus, "Here's what I'm doing. Please follow me and help me" instead of saying, "Lord, You take the lead. I'll follow You today." Jesus says to His followers, "Come, follow Me," not the other way around.

Go in the Strength You Have

The Lord tells Gideon to "go in the strength you have" and Gideon replies, "How can I save Israel? My clan is the weakest in Manasseh, and

I am the least in my family." Instead of being the best of the best, Gideon was pointing out he was the worst of the worst.

Can you relate with Gideon? Instead of feeling like you were born from a long line of happy, healthy moms, maybe you come from a dysfunctional family. Broken doesn't begin to describe it. Yet God delights in working powerfully through weak people—people like Gideon, Rahab, and Ruth to name a few from the Bible. Don't let your past family life determine your present family life. You have your own story to write.

When I first had Ethan, I had no idea how to hold a baby. I could put my hands under his little armpits and pull him in close. That was about it. Some of my friends who weren't even moms seemed so much more comfortable holding my little lump, turning him upside down and right side up and cradling him like a football. I wasn't equipped with baby know-how or born with natural instincts. I had to learn. Going in the strength that we have means coming as we are. God doesn't expect us to be like the culinary mom on our left or interior decorator mom on our right. He wants us to come as we are with all our strengths and weaknesses, and with a willing heart to learn.

God will surround you with people who can help you as a mom, if you will let them. Being teachable is a prerequisite to growth. When Noelle was about three, she would throw a fit every time I tried to wash her face. She'd jerk to the left and right, squirm and complain. It drove me nuts. But when James washed her face, she was perfectly still. She almost tilted her head back angelically while he washed her face with ease.

One day, I humbled myself and asked James, "How do you get Noelle to do that? She's never still for me."

"Oh, it's easy," James replied. "Noelle knows she can get away with that with you. But she knows I won't stand for it."

My first reaction was, "Well, *la-dee-da* for you!" But as I thought it over, I knew he was right. There was no fooling around with Daddy. Daddy means what he says. But Mommy…well, she can be pushed around. So, the next time we were at the sink, I went on the offensive with my new-found strength. "Noelle, from now on, you will treat me like you treat Daddy when we're at the sink or else you will be disciplined." She pushed me, I gave her the discipline, and our sink struggle ended after just a few encounters like that.

Part of being a mom warrior is humbling yourself and learning from others (even from your husband). Instead of hiding in the bathroom in the dark, absolutely clueless, you can step out into the light of others who have gone before you. Let these words from Karen Ehman encourage you:

> Keep showing up for duty. Every day is different. Some days are awful. Some days are wonderful. You have to tell yourself in the middle of the awful one that there will be a wonderful one coming. Statistically, they can't all be bad.
>
> If you are raising kids to find enjoyment or if you are raising kids so people think you're awesome, you're going to be able to stick with it only so far. Then you're going to want to chuck the whole thing. You're not always enjoying it. You're not always awesome. But if you truly say I'm doing this to glorify God and make His name famous, then it makes you keep going.[3]

Keep going, mighty warrior mom! But also remember to take retreats from the battlefield. Go on a women's retreat over the weekend. Plan a getaway with your husband once a year or more. Attend a moms' group or a Bible study without your children. After time away, you'll return a more energized, focused mom who doesn't want to run and hide in the bathroom at the first sight of blood.

Today's Energy Boost

Go ahead. Say it out loud: I am a mighty warrior mom. God sees me as victorious, and so do I.

Today's Prayer

Lord, thank You for seeing a champion in me. Thank You for never abandoning me. Forgive me from drifting off Your path sometimes. Help me follow You closely and to obey my orders from You. Make me into a mighty mom, a warrior who fights for her family.

Day 21

Facing Goliath

*Then the Philistine said, "This day I defy the armies of
Israel! Give me a man and let us fight each other."*
1 Samuel 17:10

One summer evening when Ethan was eight, he and James were playing basketball in our driveway against another father/son team. He
came in the house dripping with sweat. I told him to get in the shower. You
would have thought I asked him to jump in a pool filled with alligators.
He burst into tears. "Why can't I just rinse my face? I just want to go to
bed!" he pleaded. "When I'm an adult, I'm not going to take *any* showers!"

My unsympathetic response was, "Good luck with that." As I tucked
him in that night, he was still mad. "I could be asleep right now, but you
made me take a shower!" For my little boy on that hot summer night,
Goliath wasn't the six-foot dad on the basketball court. It was the dreaded
shower his mother made him take. He was challenged to obey when he
didn't want to.

The giants our children face get larger as they age. At eight, Ethan wres-
tled with personal hygiene. When he's eighteen, I think it's safe to say the
subject will be much weightier. As moms, we must fight the desire to rescue our children from any and every sign of danger or discomfort. Our
kids need to learn how to face their Goliaths on their own.

A Goliath Made of Clay

Dannah Gresh had a huge Goliath to face as a teenager: sexual sin.
Looking back now as an adult, she knows that was terribly painful for

her mom to watch. She had a mom who prayed and believed that God was going to do mighty things in her life in spite of her mistakes. God answered those prayers. Today Dannah writes and ministers to moms and daughters through her Pure Freedom ministry. Facing her Goliath has opened the door for God to use her life to touch others. Dannah says,

> If you're going to be a happy mom, you have to realize God's going to give your children Goliaths to face. You want them to have these picture perfect lives with straight As and a best friend who loves Jesus. You want them to excel in sports. You don't want them to struggle in sports or academics or with friendships. Yet when you look at your own life as a mom, the areas where God touches you most are often the areas where you struggle the most. When you give those areas to God, He can use them.

When Dannah's daughter Lexi was twelve years old, Lexi attended a pottery class in an artsy studio. Her instructor was agnostic, but Dannah didn't think much of it. After all, it was a pottery class, not a philosophy course. One night, it was clearly going to be about more than art. The gallery display in the front lobby had clay sculptures of Adam and Eve, looking very sexual and vile. The display included an old Bible with every word crossed out except for one page open in Revelation. The only three words not marked out were: God is dead.

Dannah didn't want to let Lexi attend pottery class that night. She thought about taking her out for ice cream instead. But God said no. God clearly impressed on Dannah that she could walk around the block and pray for Lexi, but that she should not take her out:

> I walked around the block that whole hour praying for her. When she came out, my twelve-year-old had been sharing her faith vibrantly with the older girl in her class who was an atheist. Most importantly, there was a younger girl there who was a Christian who was terrified of everything they were talking about. Lexi was able to comfort her. She did it in twelve-year-old style. She told me the atheist said there is no heaven and hell, to which Lexi replied, "Well, you might be right, but if there is, I know I'm not going to hell." Lexi got in the car and she was supercharged.
>
> If we're not constantly having a conversation with the Holy Spirit about our children, we will become paranoid, legalistic moms

who don't allow them to face the Goliaths that God means for them to face. When they face things you really wish they didn't have to, you can trust God knows what He is doing there. Without that, it would be really hard to be a happy mom in this world.[4]

David stood alone against Goliath. His confidence was in the living God, and he knew his cause was just. As a young shepherd, David had the experience of killing a lion and a bear while protecting his flock. His past victories helped him face his present giant. Like David, your child needs to amass a few victories to experience God's faithfulness. Instead of intervening, sometimes you need to step back and allow your child to stand alone.

When Your Giant Shows Up Everyday

At other times you will face a Goliath *together* with your child. Your giant may not only visit; he might bring his suitcase and settle in for a spell. Maybe that's how it feels if you have a child who's struggling with a learning disorder or physical disability. Dr. Jennifer Degler remembers when her son Jake was initially diagnosed with learning disorders and ADHD.

> I got a huge stack of books on learning disorders and ADHD. I probably read three books in twenty-four hours. I was totally overwhelmed. My husband came home and I was crying, surrounded by books. I looked at him and said, "We never should have propagated! What were we thinking? Our genes are bad." I was like a crazy woman. I blew it all up in my mind. I was saying things like our kindergartner is going to work at a fast-food place all his life. My husband said, "Honey, we need to put the books away."

It certainly helps to have a voice of reason to talk us off the ledge. Jennifer has since learned to train her mind to stay in the moment. Not to worry about how her kindergartner is going to make a living, but how he's going to learn to tie his shoes. She loves this quote by Elisabeth Elliot: "Today is mine. Tomorrow is none of my business. If I peer anxiously into the fog of the future, I will strain my spiritual eyes so that I will not see clearly what is required of me now."[5] Jennifer says,

It's so easy when your child has special issues to peer anxiously into the fog of the future and worry yourself sick about what will happen ten years from now. Chances are if they're doing okay as a kindergartener, they're going to do okay as a first grader. They don't have to be able to write college essays when they're five.[6]

Do Not Be "Ufred"

When I was in elementary school, I was afraid of a girl in my class. I was skinny. She was stocky. I was tall. She was taller. I was soft-spoken. She was brash. I was brainy and wore glasses. She was a jock. Get the picture? To buy peace with her, I would scratch her arm in class. She'd sit in front of me, push her arm back toward my desk, and I was supposed to scratch it on demand. The funny thing is, in time, we became friends.

Giants come in all shapes and sizes. God knew we would face giants and face fear. When Noelle was about four, her tormentor, as you may guess, was her older brother. One day, she wrote him a brave note that read: *I am not ufred uv you Ethan.*

He took the note and with great bravado, ripped it in two. As a writer mom, I quickly confiscated the torn note to keep for future reference. So remember, when a giant threatens you or your child, God is on your side. Write it for the world to see: "I am not ufred uv you, Goliath!"

Today's Energy Boost

What Goliath is your child facing today? What giant are you afraid of?

Today's Prayer

Lord, You say in Psalm 50:15, "Call on me in the day of trouble; I will deliver you, and you will honor me." I call on You now, Lord, to deliver my child from the giants that face him or her today. Maybe they are unseen giants I don't even know about. Help my child stand with You. Make his or her faith strong. Deliver me from my Goliaths. I know You will answer this prayer. Praise Your mighty name.

Thick Skin Required

*"Don't be afraid of them. Remember the Lord, who is
great and awesome, and fight for your families.*

Nehemiah 4:14

"Lucy, did you just cut my hair?"

I was sitting, minding my own business, typing away on my computer. Lucy had come behind me with her stool. She was using me as her life-size doll, combing my hair, pinning and braiding it. All of a sudden, I heard a *snip*!

I whipped around to see my preschool beautician holding a pair of scissors and one inch of my hair. She was frozen in place, caught hair-handed. It was obvious she knew she had done something terribly wrong because her face registered shock and awe.

"You feel bad about cutting my hair and you want to cry, don't you?" I said.

She began to sob. *Well,* I thought, *at least she's remorseful.* Thankfully, I have a lot of hair and the damage wasn't noticeable. I told her it was okay and that I knew she would never do that again.

On another morning, I took several hot rollers out of my hair. Lucy looked at me and said with great feeling, "That looks *horrible!* I feel sorry for you."

From the top of your bad hair day to the bottom of your weary feet, motherhood can be a rough business where thick skin is required.

No More Softies

Moms have earned the reputation for being the softies in the house. We're sentimental, softhearted people who can be easily manipulated by needy boys and girls. There's certainly a place for this mommy tenderness, but the problem lies in its overuse. Many times our kids need toughness not tenderness.

When the girls aren't in school, they love to come with me to exercise class. Noelle woke up early and was all ready to join me, but Lucy was dawdling at breakfast and hadn't brushed her teeth. Noelle and I headed out the door without her. She burst into tears, "Please, Mommy! Please, Mommy! Let me come!" She followed us through the garage, crying in the driveway. "Please, please, let me come!"

Can you guess what I did? Yes, I left without her. She had to stay home with James. I knew the experience of being left behind would be a powerful teacher. If she wanted to come, she needed to get ready faster. At class, one of the moms asked where Lucy was. I told her about Lucy's tears and pleading in the driveway. My friend said, "Oh, I couldn't have done that. I would have taken her. I can go pick her up right now." Softie alert! In the moment, it's easier to give in to our children's tears instead of standing tough.

Like the time Ethan said to me, "You're the meanest mom!"

He was in a huff because we were running late to one of his favorite activities: dinner at Baba and Nana's. (When Ethan was a baby, he couldn't say "grandpa" so he said "baba," and it stuck.) The kids were going to take baths at my parents' house after dinner. But then Noelle said she wanted to take hers at home, and I figured that would save my parents a little effort.

Ethan went crazy. "She's going to make us late if she takes a bath first!"

He huffed and puffed, changing my happy home quickly into a war zone. As calmly as I could, I sat Ethan down and said, "You can't ruin everyone's evening because you are upset."

"I was born grumpy," he said.

When it was time for eight-year-old grumpy to get into the car, I told him when he got out of the car, he better snap out of it or else his sisters would be going to Nana's and he would be coming back home. That's what triggered him to say, "You're the meanest mom!" That ugliness was followed by "I wish you weren't coming in for dinner. I wish you could beam yourself back home and disappear."

Ouch. I told him flatly *my* parents had invited *me* to dinner also. When the door to the house opened, I acted as if nothing out of the ordinary had transpired. Within about a minute, Ethan was back to himself. I think the teriyaki chicken, sourdough bread, and dessert helped bring him to his senses, along with his mean mom. After dinner, Ethan invited me to play a game with everyone.

"No, I don't have to play," I said. "I know you don't want me to be here."

"That's not true," he said. "But I guess I said that earlier."

He knew he had acted badly. A grand apology would have been nicer, but that was enough for me in that moment. John Rosemond in *The Well-Behaved Child* writes a word of encouragement to us mean moms:

> This is about being a "mean" parent, but I'm not talking about being cruel, hateful, spiteful, or sadistic. I'm talking about saying what you mean and meaning what you say. In that light, one of the greatest compliments your child can give you is to tell you that you are "mean."[7]

Other Mean Moms

Sometimes you don't just need thick skin to endure the things your child says. Sometimes you need a rawhide exterior for the mean things other moms say. Rhonda Rhea remembers the challenge of raising her children as pastor's kids. They were parenting in a fishbowl, under scrutiny, living family life in front of an audience.

> One time a lady came to me and said, "Your son did such and such. You know I would have expected more from the pastor's child." I didn't get mad. I just said, nice and calmly, "You know what, he's just a kid. And I would appreciate it if you would let him be just a kid because being a pastor's kid didn't give him a special dispensation of grace. It didn't make him sinless any more than being a pastor's wife has made me sinless!" She said, "You know I hadn't really thought of that."
>
> That woman ended up being an advocate for me. She got the word out—let the pastor's kid be a kid. It won't always turn out that way. Some people are going to be jerks about it. But the calm response is the godly response. We might be tempted to key their car later, but that's probably not the best way—ha![8]

You know the power words have. Use them carefully with your children and other moms. Be cautious and zealous to guard your words, but on the flipside, be gracious and forgiving when someone says something that rubs you the wrong way. In her book *Keep It Shut*, Karen Ehman writes:

> Lysa TerKeurst is the president of Proverbs 31 Ministries, the organization for which I write and speak. She drew up a wonderful guideline for all of us as we interact with each other doing ministry together. When dealing with others, she declares, we should believe the best before we assume the worst. So when a conflict arises or our feathers get ruffled, we shouldn't automatically jump to the conclusion that the other person meant us ill, but give them the benefit of the doubt. Not assume the worst, but believe the best about their motives.[9]

So the next time you feel like crumbling under the criticism of a mean mom, fall to your knees instead. Ask God to help you forgive others who hurt you and to hear what criticisms are valid and helpful. Seek to have thick skin and a tender heart.

Don't Let Go

I love the story Fern Nichols tells about a mother's will to fight and hold on, no matter the cost. While on vacation at a beach house with her family, a little girl ran into the ocean for a swim. Her mother was watching from the house and saw a shark's fin in the distance. Frantically running toward her daughter, she yelled for her daughter to swim to shore. Just as the mother reached her girl, the shark attacked, grabbing the girl's legs. The mom grabbed her daughter's arm and would not let go. The six-foot-long shark was much stronger, but the mom would not let go. A fisherman who happened to be nearby heard the mom's screams, pulled out a rifle, and shot the shark.

The little girl survived. On her arms were deep scars where her mother's fingernails had dug into her flesh to pull her away from the shark. A reporter came to interview her in the hospital and asked to see her scars on her legs from the shark. But then the little girl said, "I have great scars on my arms too. I have them because my mom wouldn't let go."[11]

A Word for Stepmoms from Laura Petherbridge

The best way to be a smart stepmom with a smile on your face is to first accept and embrace the fact that this is going to be different than a first-time family. Some of the stepmoms that struggle the most are those who are constantly trying to make the stepfamily think, look, and act like a first-time family. Letting go of the dream, the Brady Bunch thinking you had before you got married, is one of the crucial steps of becoming a happy stepmom. You've got to lay down the things that are not realistic. Recognize you can have a happy stepfamily, but not if you keep trying to force everyone into a format that is not going to work. My grown stepsons call me their dad's wife, Laura. So many stepmoms are offended by that, but that's what I am. I'm their father's wife.

Almost all experts agree, the stepparent's role, particularly in the first years of marriage, is to not be in the disciplinary role for their stepchild. Authority comes over time. When we're born into a family, our parents are automatic authorities. But a stepparent doesn't get automatic authority in the mind of a child, so it's important for the stepmom to recognize that the kids' dad needs to be the disciplinarian. The exception to this rule is the stepmom of young children who needs to be able to discipline if she's the only parental role for the majority of time.[10]

What a story! Fern says,

> As long as our children have breath, we pray. We will not let go. We ask God that they would love Him and be devoted to Him. We pray that our children would fulfill the destiny of God's will in their lives. We will not let go, especially in the teen years when we're not seeing any of that happening. We will still pray according to God's Word and we will not let go.[12]

Do you know what the antonym of softie is? Powerhouse. It's time for powerhouse moms to rise up who will not let go, give in, give up, let up, shut down, or shut up. Keep your heart tender, be thick-skinned, and never walk out of the spiritual battle for your child's soul.

Today's Energy Boost

Picture yourself coated in Teflon. Whatever your child says today to hurt or manipulate you will not stick. Wash off any icky comments and move on.

Today's Prayer

Lord, help me to persevere when I am tempted to give up or give in. Mold me into a leader for my children. I don't want to be swayed or persuaded by my child's folly. Give me thick skin and a tender heart. May my mouth not lead me into sin. Instead, please keep a watch over the door of my lips.

Day 23

That's Entertainment

All the days of the oppressed are wretched,
but the cheerful heart has a continual feast.

Proverbs 15:15

It was my first time meeting with the sales director and the VP of marketing at the publishing house for my first book. Think power breakfast in the big leagues. And do you know what I introduced as the first topic of conversation? "My husband, James, took our two-year-old daughter to the bathroom this morning, and she went number two for the first time in the toilet!"

Yes, I really said that.

Our daily lives as moms are filled with the laughable, absurd, quotable, darling, hilarious, and at times downright crude. Today I want to challenge you to find the funny in it all. If you look around with a light heart and eyes wide open, you'll find plenty of material for hours of standup comedy.

Like the time I dumped the clean laundry on my bed. Lucy came by and asked if she could have a laundry-sorting job like her older siblings. I showed her a pair of my underwear and told her to sort out my underwear and put them in a pile. She held up a pair with a brown leopard pattern and said in her two-year-old voice, "Are dees your speakin' undawear?" Laughing, I asked her why she thought that. "Cuz they are brown like your speakin' clothes."

Another time, Lucy and I were having lunch together. She told me, "When I hurt myself, I say *comforter*! And that's you. You come." My mommy heart soared. Then she added, "Because you are so warm and fat," which, of course, brought me right back down to earth.

Ethan called the chocolate malt balls "Whoopers" instead of "Whoppers." Lucy insisted on being called "Cinderwella." I'm sure you have a list of these funny sayings too if your children are young. Write them down while you remember. Keep a journal of funny moments with your kids.

Better Than Medicine

It says in Proverbs 17:22 that "a cheerful heart is good medicine, but a crushed spirit dries up the bones." Here we see the correlation between our inward life and our physical and mental health. This verse is about our ability to persevere through the years. The word *medicine* occurs only here in the Old Testament. A crushed spirit refers to being depressed or sad.[13] Depression is a real struggle for many moms. Nearly one in four women ages fifty to sixty-four take an antidepressant, with 13 percent of the overall population in the US on antidepressants.[14] That's more than one in ten people who struggle enough with depression to take medication. Too many of us are not experiencing the health in one's bones mentioned several times in Proverbs.

The Bible gives us an antidote to depression, sadness, and deteriorating health: a cheerful heart. A happy heart. Other translations say a merry heart. The idea here is someone who is delightful, full of festivity and high spirits, and joyous. Don't worry if you feel too Eeyore-like to fit this description. Chances are you have some kids around who can help you laugh more frequently.

When I was pregnant with Lucy, I was tired all the time. I remember apologizing to Ethan because I didn't have the energy to volunteer in his class.

"That's okay, Mommy," he said. "You can do it after the baby is bigger. No problem."

Noelle chimed in, "I will be your doctor and help you and your baby. I will get a stick and pull your baby out."

Sometimes the lifeline out of fatigue and the doldrums comes through the funny comments of our children. That is, if we make the point to notice and cherish those moments.

You've got to find the entertainment value in your everyday life—even when it's at your expense. James is the baker in our home. Killer chocolate-chip cookies are synonymous with Daddy. One day he was in the kitchen caramelizing butter, and the kids were dusted in flour. As I walked into the kitchen, James, whose nickname is Dubba, said in a singsong voice, "When it's got to be good, it's got to be Dubba." To which Ethan quickly added, "And if it's got to be bad, it's got to be Mama!" We laughed then, and we still laugh about that now. Sure, at the time I said, "Oh, Ethan, don't be so mean." He replied with great feeling, "It's the truth!" Well, we all know I write books...I don't bake cookies.

Fun Seekers

Talk about living up to a name. If you've ever met speaker and author Kendra Smiley, you know she married into the right family. She remembers when her firstborn returned home from the first day of kindergarten.

"Mom," he said, "there's someone in our class with the funniest name!"

"What's that, honey?" Kendra asked.

"Her last name is *Pancake!*"

"I know you don't understand this now, but our last name is funny too. We don't make fun of other people's names," Kendra said.

Kendra's three sons are all grown up now. One of her boys reminded her that whenever she wanted the kids to get in the car, she never said, "Let's get in the car." Instead she'd call out, "C'mon, fun seekers! It's time to go!" I love the anticipation she created for her family. A trip to the dentist could be an adventure! Kendra, the fun chairman, says:

> For married couples, there's usually one person who finds joy more easily. You need balance. Every family needs an adult. Two might be overkill. My husband, John, is the adult in our home. We never said, "Are we having too much fun?" We looked for how we could make an ordinary mundane day into something that brought joy into people's lives.[15]

Rhonda Rhea is another woman who is adept at seeing the humorous side of life:

> You need to embrace your own personality. Not all of us are belly laughers. You can keep a pleasant attitude without cracking up every three seconds. Get off your case and settle for pleasant. We

have to take into account how God wired us. Some of us are not really wired to be constantly falling over laughing. Now, I *am* one of those—there are several shorts in the wiring—I see a lot of humor where there isn't any.

For the mom who is struggling to see the more pleasant side of things, remember there will be good days and not-so-good days. Make staying in God's Word your number one priority. If you try to stay plugged into joy throughout the day, and you're trying to do that yourself, that's not going to work so well. Instead, be fueled by the Word of God. Read Philippians for a while, a letter full of joy even though it was written in prison. That's even harder than motherhood. Well, maybe not a whole lot harder on some days, but still harder![16]

You can feel trapped as a parent, stuck in a seven-by-seven room with a screaming toddler or moody teen. Yet even on those kinds of days, you can find something to laugh about if you look.

Ethan Looks for Thomas

When Ethan was two, like most boys, he loved all things transportation. Thomas the Train was his very favorite. For a treat, he would watch Thomas the Train DVDs. He couldn't pronounce *Thomas* so he called him *Mom-mus*. When the movie *Cars* came out, we decided to give the big screen a try with our little tot. Ethan lasted about two minutes through the previews before he cried, "*Out*! I want *out* of here!"

We exited the dark movie theatre and stepped into the hallway. Ethan walked up and down the hall saying, "Mom-mus, where are you?" He turned left and right, checking the doors and posters for any sign of "Mom-mus."

He never found Thomas that day—and we didn't see *Cars* on the big screen. But that experience was still highly entertaining to me. Many times the laughs don't come when everything goes right. They come when everything goes wrong.

Bloom where you're planted. Laugh in times of sun and rain—and you will enjoy a perpetual feast that will nourish you through the long haul.

Today's Energy Boost

Watch a clip of our family's favorite comedian, Tim Hawkins, at www.timhawkins.net. Guaranteed to make you laugh!

Today's Prayer

The Bible says the joy of the Lord is our strength. Lord, please fill me with Your joy. Highlight the funny things in my day so I will notice them. Help me not to take myself too seriously. Stamp out any depression in my family. I rejoice in Your goodness, faithfulness, and kindness to me today.

Day 24

Finding Someone to Follow

Guide older women into lives of reverence so they end up
as neither gossips nor drunks, but models of goodness. By
looking at them, the younger women will know how to love
their husbands and children, be virtuous and pure, keep a
good house, be good wives. We don't want anyone looking
down on God's Message because of their behavior.

Titus 2:3-5 (MSG)

I was reading a pink book with big lips on it, which got Lucy's attention. "What are you reading, Mom?" I was reading *Keep It Shut: What to Say, How to Say It, and When to Say Nothing At All* by Karen Ehman. I replied, "A book about controlling yourself." Lucy twirled around with a Cinderella-dreamy look in her eyes. "Oh, I love to control myself!"

In her mind, she may think self-control is a snap. But we all know self-control is an ongoing struggle for all of us—including my five-year-old. That's why motherhood works better when you have an older, wiser mom to look up to.

Even if you have a full-time job outside the home, consider motherhood as your profession. You are the president of Moms, Inc. at your residence. Who would you want on your board of directors? What moms model good character and strong leadership? Who has respectful children? Who has a strong marriage? Maybe you don't know anyone in your sphere of friendships who doesn't yell at her kids or fight with her husband. Get creative and have mom mentors through books, podcasts, and radio programs. *Focus on the Family* and *Family Life Today* are my favorite programs for sound parenting advice.

Although my James is obviously not a mom, he has observed many moms thrive when they have a mentor, someone to look up to and follow. He says,

> Find role models and be with them. Figure out what they do differently. You'll be amazed at what they define as normal because it's different than what most families do. For instance, I stopped by a client's house and saw their four young kids eating enormous pieces of broccoli and spinach at the dinner table. Each child's serving of vegetables was equal to what my entire family would eat. Wow, their normal diet was not our normal diet. It was inspiring! Find good role models and hang out with them. Let their good habits rub off on you.

Get a Coach

We know about soccer coaches and baseball coaches, but what about mom coaches? In the same way a coach extracts the best from her players, a coach can help us as moms rise to the occasion and hold us accountable when we lose our way. When we want to throw in the towel, a coach can say, "It's going to be all right. Tomorrow's a new day."

Kristen Welch remembers the impact an older mom had on her. This mom volunteered weekly for Mercy House, Kristen's nonprofit organization in Kenya. Kristen says,

> I had an argument with my teen on the way to school. I was really broken about it. We were still mad when she went to school. When I opened the door to the Mercy House office, my mom friend was sitting there. She asked if I got the kids to school. I proceeded to throw up all my parenting woes on her. I started crying and I asked her, "Is this normal? You've raised daughters." I needed someone to tell me this was normal.
>
> That's exactly what she did. She told me everything I was experiencing—my daughter's desire for freedom and my desire to keep her little—was completely normal. It was the most freeing sentence anyone could have said to me. All moms experience these questions, challenges, and feelings of regret. One of the most practical ways to keep going is to realize you are not alone.[17]

Sometimes a coach is needed for comfort and sometimes he or she is needed for correction. While reading *The Well-Behaved Child* by psychologist John Rosemond, one section stood out to me. It was about how we tack "okay?" to the end of our instructions to our children. For example, "I need to use this room to talk to a friend of mine who's coming over in a few minutes. How about let's get these toys picked up now, okay?" Rosemond writes,

> What does that mean? If it's not *okay* with her child, he doesn't have to do it? I once challenged parents, through my syndicated newspaper column, to count the number of times they tacked "…okay?" onto the end of a supposed instruction to their kids… Yes, bad habits are hard to break, but they can be broken. Here's how: before giving an instruction to your child, ask yourself: "What do I want my child to do, and how can I phrase it in the most authoritative way possible, using the least number of words?"[18]

Wouldn't you know it, the very next morning I heard myself say to Lucy on the way to kindergarten, "I don't want you to chase that boy around the playground. He doesn't like that. If he pushes you, it's your own fault for not giving him space. So don't chase him, *okay?*" I said the very thing I had promised to purge from my vocabulary the night before. Not that Lucy fully understood my personal mom training-in-progress, but I corrected myself. "Lucy, do not chase that boy on the playground today." Period. End of sentence. Stop talking.

Now my "okay?" alert is on. I can improve my leadership skills at home by eliminating that tag on my instructions. Legendary coach John Wooden said, "A coach is someone who can give correction without causing resentment."[19] Find older moms and parenting experts you can follow and respect. Your mother load will be much lighter as a result.

Grandma Did Know Best

Would your grandmother have tolerated your mom sassing back, playing hours of video games while the chores went undone, or refusing to eat the food she served? Probably not. Although our world marches forward in technology, it's going backward in regard to the home. The quality of family life is rapidly declining.

Promise to My Teenagers by Kristen Welch

I will not beg, yell or force you to see things my way.

I will try to see things your way.

I won't ask you to do something I won't do.

I won't pick a battle over things that don't matter.

I will cry with you, even when you don't see my tears.

I will wait up when I long to sleep.

I will pray when I want to worry.

I will give you privacy, when I want to intrude.

I will let you sleep until noon (occasionally).

I will hush when I want to talk.

I will apologize when I am wrong.

I will trust you.

I will get in your business if you're in danger or if you make bad decisions.

I will ask questions that make you uncomfortable.

I will let you ask me questions that make me uncomfortable.

I will listen.

I will try to fight for you and not with you.

When the world expects you to fail, to fall away, to forget your roots, I will expect more.

And when you do fail, I will be the first one at your side.

I will love you no matter what.

Most of all, when I mess up and forget or break these promises, I will try again. We will try again.

No matter how tall you grow or how far you go, I am your mother. *I will be here.*[20]

John Rosemond comments about America breaking with established child-rearing traditions in the late sixties and early seventies:

> We headed down a path described to us by psychologists and other mental health professionals. We ought to be waking up at this point to the fact that this new child rearing has been disastrous for children. It's been disastrous for the American marriage and the American school.

Today's children, when compared with children in the fifties, even accounting for reporting error, are ten times more likely by age sixteen to experience a serious emotional setback. Traditional parenting wasn't perfect, because there's nothing human beings can do to be universally perfect. But there is validity to the idea that it was better. This is something people resist because this is a very progressive time in history. People are skeptical to the idea that there was anything better about the so-called good old days. But all the statistics on child mental health indicate that children in the fifties were mentally and emotionally sturdier than today's kids.

The fifth commandment in the Ten Commandments is the only commandment that comes with a promise. "Honor your father and your mother, so that you may live long in the land the LORD your God is giving you" (Exodus 20:12). John Rosemond continues:

> What that means in part is that by carrying on family traditions and adhering to fundamental traditional understandings of how a family should operate…when this is multiplied by millions of families, this is how you stabilize, perpetuate and sustain culture. It's so vitally important to the strength of any culture that its child-rearing traditions are perpetuated from one generation to the next. Those child-rearing traditions in the final analysis define the culture.[21]

Perhaps it's time to toss a few modern parenting ideas aside and take your grandmother out to lunch instead. Our culture will thrive when children honor their elders, not when they can boss them around.

Today's Energy Boost

Count the number of times you tack on "okay?" to your instructions to your children. Make it your goal to eliminate that word from your mom repertoire.

Today's Prayer

Show me, Lord, who I can have on my Moms, Inc. board of directors. Who are the women and parenting experts in my life I can follow, who will guide me to become a more godly and happy mom? Help me to receive correction because I know You love those You discipline.

Day 25

You're Not Raising Kids

Start children off on the way they should go,
and even when they are old they will not turn from it.

PROVERBS 22:6

Y ou could hang a sign over your front door that reads "Job Training in Progress." It could serve as a warning to guests in the same way a "Student Driver" sign cautions you on the road. You see, every day you are training your child to become an adult. Erma Bombeck said it this way, "I take a very practical view of raising children. I put a sign in each of their rooms: 'Checkout Time is 18 years.'"[22]

You've heard terms like *failure to launch, prolonged adolescence, preadulthood.* When your children reach their twenties, you don't want to be packing their lunches and filling out their job applications (and mailing them out too). You want them to function as responsible adults. It all begins with a mommy mindset that says, "I am not raising a child. I am raising an *adult.*" There is a difference. One takes a short view; the other takes the long. If you are raising a child, your job training revolves around entertainment, comfort, cartoons, lollipops, and interdependence. If you're raising an adult, it revolves around responsibility, character, discipline, good old-fashioned hard work, and independence.

Rhonda Rhea has five twentysomethings of her own. Rhonda has noticed some disturbing trends with her kids' peers.

> You see a lot of seniors graduate from high school. They're getting ready to go to college and they have no foundation for making decisions on their own. They've never dealt with their own failures or consequences. Parents can pretty easily send off their

children to college, ill-equipped for facing the world. You see college kids slip into all kinds of bad behaviors because they are manipulated by their peers. They never really learned how to make their own decisions and stand for what they believe and deal with difficulties on their own.

My friend Marie didn't know how to do her laundry as a college student (I didn't either). She remembers having to call her mom to ask how to use the coin machines. That made quite an impression on her. Now that Marie is a mom herself, she wants her kids to be equipped to cook, clean, and do laundry—and she's not waiting until college. She has her one-year-old making her bed. I know, a one-year-old can't make her bed, but she can hang her blanket over the crib before getting out. What a great way to begin teaching a baby good habits that will serve her as a future adult. It's never too early to start.

No Easy Passes

We want our children to feel loved and special. As mama bears, we're there to protect and rescue. But there comes a point when we have to back away and let them take the heat for their own actions. Rhonda Rhea has this caution:

> We can train our children to be irresponsible. *If I forget that, my mom will run it to me. If I forget my homework, my mom will bring it to school.* You have to let them learn from consequences even when it's due to them just being a scatterbrain. Sometimes, you may bail them out to show them grace and mercy, like Jesus does for us. But let your kids know they should never expect that.

With job training to become an adult in mind, here's a letter I wrote to Noelle's second-grade teacher:

Dear Mrs. E,

Noelle is late today because she didn't finish her breakfast or brush her teeth on time. We've given her plenty of time to complete her morning activities and want to teach her there is a consequence to moving so slowly. Feel free to give her extra homework or keep her in for recess.

Sincerely,
Arlene Pellicane

When I picked Noelle up from school that day, I knew instantly that reality-based consequences were working their magic.

"How was your day?" I asked my dejected student.

"You know," she said sadly.

I drew her in for a hug, and she burst into tears—the kind that made her shoulders shake and her face turn beet red.

Turns out the day kept going downhill for her at school. She got a yellow, which is the warning color for misbehavior. Noelle typically brings home blues or greens for good or excellent behavior.

"I was doing the talking," she said in between sobs. "I'm sorry. My friends weren't talking to me. It was my fault. I was talking to *them*."

Now it was my turn to read the note from Mrs. E:

> *Dear Mrs. Pellicane,*
>
> *Thank you for letting me know about Noelle's tardy. She had extra homework since she missed the problem of the day. Today she is on yellow because she continued to talk and play with another student on the carpet during our writing lesson, even after a warning. Noelle usually does not need reminders about her behavior. Thank you for all your support!*

There's a verse in the Bible that says, "Godly sorrow brings repentance that leads to salvation and leaves no regret" (2 Corinthians 7:10). I could see that Noelle was genuinely repentant. She confessed and took responsibility for her wrongdoing at school. She was maturing—as a second grader—and learning how to deal with failure and start again.

Someday They Will Launch

When Rhonda Rhea's children turned twelve or thirteen, she would do something special for that child related to his or her interests. One child went to Haiti on a missions trip. Another went to a writers' conference. Rhonda created an opportunity for her kids to learn about whatever they were interested in for a future career. It was a milestone for Rhonda to say, "I will treat you as an adult from here on out as far as you will let me." She told her kids:

> If you start acting like a kid, I will treat you like a kid and go into *mega mother mode*! But if you will allow it, we can start building

what will eventually become our friendship. The more you allow, the more we'll be able to do that. I'm going to let you make your own decisions and treat you like an adult. You have to obey the rules of the house and to respect your family members. I have to do that too!

This talk meant Rhonda had to bite her lip when her daughters came up with some really weird hairstyles. "I did tell my friends," Rhonda said, "because I didn't want them to think I was a bad mother. The bonus is that in the future, I'll get to pull out those pictures and make merciless fun of my children."[23]

Gwen Smith passes along these wise words about raising kids who have a sense of mission:

> As they get older, there are layers of maturity I see in my children. In Matthew 10, we read about Jesus telling His disciples to go out in pairs to tell others the kingdom of heaven was near. He gave them full authority. There's a model there for us as mothers. I need to empower my children to live their lives. They're not mine. They're God's. Whether their mission is to go to school or the store, they need to feel my courage and confidence in them. Our fear can limit them. Jesus promised hard times and opposition to His disciples. But He also said that when they were dragged before rulers to testify, not to worry. He would give them the words to say.
>
> How do we release our children into the world? How did Jesus do it? He didn't hunker down with His twelve disciples. He sent them out. Bad things are going to happen. But when they happen, don't worry, God's got this. The more we tether ourselves to the heart and mission of God, the more our confidence will grow. Look at Jesus and how He treated His disciples. That's what our children are. They are the people we are raising up to love and serve God.[24]

When Ethan was in kindergarten, he broke his leg. Not on the playground. Not at school. But right in the comfort of his own home. You know he suffered only a few bruises getting hit by a car while riding his bike. He wasn't so fortunate against our stationary exercise bike. He was pedaling super fast, and then he took his legs off the pedals. Boom! The speeding pedal struck him right on the shin.

Six weeks in a cast was a hard sentence for a five-year-old. It turned out to be hard for me too—from caring for Ethan at home to visiting his class daily to take him on bathroom breaks. But do you know what? I would not trade that experience. In his kindergarten class, I was astounded to see several children serving Ethan. When he hobbled toward a chair, three kids would pop up to push a chair underneath him. At recess, one quiet boy ran ahead to hold the door open every day for Ethan to pass through. The kids would engage Ethan in "races" at recess. They would run slowly to make it competitive. Truly, I saw the best being brought out in others and in my son too. *Patience. Endurance. Contentment. Gratitude. Resilience. Discipline.* Even though we'd like to shelter our children from the broken legs of life, they are often their greatest teachers—and ours too.

After all, we're not raising children. We're raising adults.

Today's Energy Boost

I love what Rhonda Rhea says: "I think once my kids have kids, I'm going to look so smart. I'm going to look like the most brilliant person. I am waiting for that day!" Smile…that day will come for you too!

Today's Prayer

Lord, help me to see the big picture and to persevere. I'm not raising a child; I am raising an adult. May my son or daughter be Your servant. I pray my children will walk in truth, wisdom, and joy. May nothing shake their faith in You. Let them learn and understand the lessons You have for them today. And may I learn those lessons too.

HEALTHY

ACTION-ORIENTED

PRAYERFUL

PERSEVERANT

Becoming YES-FILLED

Day 26

Yes to Mommy Liberation

Their children will be mighty in the land;
the generation of the upright will be blessed.

PSALM 112:2

It was our little bedtime ritual. As Ethan got into his bed each night, I
would bring him a clean pair of white socks. I'd grab one sock and put
his foot in it. Then I'd do the same with his other foot. One day, when
Ethan was in *fifth* grade, I realized, *Ethan is too old for me to be putting his
socks on for him. What am I doing?*

"I don't know why I'm still putting these socks on your feet at bedtime,"
I said. "You are old enough to do it yourself from now on."

"But I like it when you do it. My servant!" he said with a laugh.

I threw a pair of socks in his face, and he's been putting on his own
socks ever since. But I have to admit I still take out the socks from the
closet and throw them on his bed. Maybe by next year I'll be able to let
go of that habit.

Many times it's not our children who have a hard time assuming more
roles and responsibilities around the house. The problem lies with *us*. We
don't want to let go of the feeling of being needed and important. As if
the earth could not continue on its axis without our involvement. We
complain about being stressed out and pulled and tugged to do every little single thing that revolves around our children, yet we're the ones who
engineer the dependence. There's good news if you are willing to hear it.
Your deliverance awaits.

The Truth About The Good Mommy Club

John Rosemond says once women have children, they begin unwittingly subscribing to the doctrine of what he calls The Good Mommy Club. This doctrine includes such ideas as:

- The Good Mommy pays as much attention to her child as she possibly can.

- The Good Mommy does for her child as much as she possibly can.

- The Good Mommy drives her child to as many developmentally enriching afterschool activities as she possibly can.

- The Good Mommy helps her child with homework every night so that he takes flawless papers back to school.

- The Good Mommy solves all of her child's problems.

This sounds about right. Or does it? Rosemond says:

> It's my contention that parenting is not stressful if you have a clear understanding of responsibility toward your child. Subscription to The Good Mommy Club guarantees a woman is going to experience the raising of children as highly stressful. Thus the complaints that are ubiquitous in American culture today from women: *This is wearing me out. This is the hardest thing I've ever done.* When I hear that from a woman, I often point out her grandma may have raised three to four times as many children as she is raising and would have never said that. The raising of children was not unusually stressful or taking any sort of daily emotional toll on her. Therefore the stress this modern mom feels doesn't have to do with children per se. It has to do with her understanding of her responsibilities toward her kids.

> Membership in The Good Mommy Club is extremely limiting to a woman. It renders her into nothing more than a servant to her children. And they do not develop a lot of respect for her. They take her for granted. They learn to manipulate her emotionally. It sets the stage for adults, and especially adult males, who don't have a lot of respect for women.

The truth is The Good Mommy Club puts the emphasis on the wrong things. It leads a woman to believe she must do *more* for her kids when really, she should do *less*. As a mom dethrones her children from the center of her universe, her children learn how to become independent and responsible. They learn mommy has a life outside of pouring milk, running a taxi service, signing permission slips, and checking temperatures.

Recently, James wanted to try out a small group at church to meet other couples. This was something new to our weekly schedule and meant the kids would go into childcare at church while we went to someone's home on Friday nights. The first two weeks were rough. The kids complained, "Do we have to go? We want to stay home. We wish we didn't have to go."

If I buy into the doctrine of The Good Mommy Club, I might say to James, "Honey, you know the kids don't like it. I feel sorry for them. I don't blame them for wanting to stay home after a long week of school. Maybe this isn't the right time to join a group." But what does that communicate to the children? *If you complain about something, you might get out of it. If you don't like something, you don't have to do it.* Last time I checked, the real world doesn't operate that way.

Perhaps more importantly, it gives decision-making power to the kids instead of us parents. James reminded me and the kids of the many, many times he remembers as a boy going to a babysitter because his parents were going out or his mom was taking a course. He didn't like it one bit, but it simply wasn't an option to refuse. As a child, he was inconvenienced regularly in order for his parents to do what they needed to do.

Somehow we've allowed the pecking order to get all mixed up. We'll bend over backward to get a child to practice, create an over-the-top birthday party, or sit through endless hours of ice skating, piano, or gymnastics. But heaven forbid our children be inconvenienced once in a while for *our* sake.

As you may have guessed, we continued going to that small group for couples. The kids learned not to complain and even started enjoying themselves. Supporting James's desire to go to the group strengthened our marriage and oneness. John Rosemond explains the ill effect of The Good Mommy Club on a marriage:

Membership in The Good Mommy Club causes a woman to over-focus on her children to the neglect of her marriage. I'm convinced this is a major contributor to male infidelity and to the high divorce rate in America.

My advice to women is simple. The covenant relationship is not the mother-child relationship. The covenant relationship in the family is that of husband and wife. If you put that relationship first and you function primarily as wife in your family, then you will be a better mother. Nothing puts a more solid foundation of security and wellbeing under a child's feet than the knowledge that his parents are in a committed relationship.

John Rosemond's mission is twofold: mother liberation and marriage restoration. Sign me up for that! Those are core values I can get behind. How about you?

International Mommy-Take-a-Day-Off Day

If you're a little sore about The Good Mommy Club because you sense a wee bit of conviction, don't tune out. John has an exercise for you to complete on a nonschool day. First thing in the morning, tell your children this is International Mommy-Take-a-Day-Off Day. On this holiday, you are not able to do anything for your children other than fix their meals and provide basic supervision. You are not able to play with them or sit down and talk. You can answer yes and no questions, but that's it. You will be completely ignoring your children all day long. If your children ask for your attention, simply say, "I'm really sorry, but today is International Mommy-Take-a-Day-Off Day. You'll have to wait until tomorrow for that." John says,

> At the end of the day, ask yourself: Are the kids okay? Did they collapse into little heaps of psychological dysfunction at 3:00 p.m.? The answer is the kids are fine. Use this exercise to begin bringing some benevolent neglect into your children's lives. Begin meeting your own needs more effectively and help your children stand on their own two feet. You can have this holiday once a month if you'd like. I often get the feedback that once the holiday occurs, International Mommy-Take-a-Day-Off Day is happening nearly every day. Kids are happy and playing on their

own. They are occupying themselves and solving their own problems. Life goes on, and it not only goes on, but it's a better life for everyone concerned.[1]

No more waiting on your kids hand and foot. No more putting white socks on for fifth graders at bedtime. No more making three different meals at dinnertime to suit everyone's taste. It's time for mommy liberation! Are you in?

Today's Energy Boost

Put your first International Mommy-Take-a-Day-Off Day on the calendar. Good! Now you have something to look forward to. Tell your spouse or a friend about this new holiday and then report back on what you learn from the day.

Today's Prayer

Lord, I know I am to train my child so he or she can be independent someday. Forgive me for being too involved, too particular, or too overbearing. Show me the stress I am creating for myself by depending on my child to give me meaning in life. Teach me how to give my children more responsibility and to make positive changes. I don't want to be part of The Good Mommy Club anymore. Bless my marriage and my children for Your glory today.

Day 27

Yes to Ignoring the Joneses

Therefore, my dear brothers and sisters, stand firm. Let nothing move you. Always give yourselves fully to the work of the Lord, because you know that your labor in the Lord is not in vain.

1 Corinthians 15:58

I reach inside Lucy's backpack for her kindergarten homework folder and look at the manila envelope with her week's reading sheet. *Hmm...I wonder how she's doing compared to the rest of the class.* I ask another parent what her daughter is reading. Yikes, I discover she's reading paragraphs while Lucy is reading only sentences. So the epic struggle to keep up with the Joneses begins in kindergarten (or sooner).

As this goes through my mind, I notice another little girl pull out her folder. *Oh, good!* Peering over her shoulder, I see she's still working on individual letters and their sounds. That makes me feel a lot better about Lucy's progress. After all, Lucy is reading *sentences.*

I know that may sound terrible, but let's be honest—we want our kids to be the cream of the crop, the top of their class, ahead of the pack. While there's nothing wrong with striving for excellence (in fact, it's to be desired), there is something wrong with constantly comparing our kids with others. As Erma Bombeck said, "Before you try to keep up with the Joneses, be sure they're not trying to keep up with you."[2]

No Race to Replicate

Maybe your kids go to public school but your best friend homeschools. You feel guilty for not being as patient or proactive as she is. Or maybe your kids don't participate in a variety of sports and you're wondering if that's wrong. We tend to look around at other families to gauge how we are scoring on the Mommy Meter. Karen Ehman reminds us we are not in a race to replicate:

> Close your eyes and quit looking at other moms and other kids. Quit looking at other marriages. The more I looked at others, the less I liked my life. Look to others for advice and encouragement. Make sure you're finding people who are real and will tell you the true story and shoot straight. Look for advice, but let go of the race to replicate someone else's experience as a mom.
>
> I can say that because I ran hard in the race to replicate when I was first a mom. I was surrounded by some really amazing mothers who had twice the number of children and their kids just all seemed to be so perfect. I felt like I needed to do exactly what they did to ensure my kids were perfect too. But my kids didn't fit the mold. None of them went with the program. The less I tried to make my kids act like other people's kids and the more I celebrated how God made them, the happier I became.[3]

Let me give you permission to ignore the Joneses. Don't live your life by another family's playbook. Create your own family distinctives by deciding what's important to you. Author Ruth Schwenk says the rhythms you set in your life are based off priorities—not someone else's, but yours.

> Your priorities inform the things you should and should not be a part of. In our culture, we're so wired that a daughter needs to do ballet, piano, and soccer. A son needs to do baseball and all these things. Understand you don't have to do everything just because someone else is doing it. I love sports, but you have to ask what's going to be more beneficial to your kids? Spending family time together or running here, there, and everywhere?
>
> We have four kids and they each choose one sport a year if they want to. But if the sport means practicing four nights a week, that doesn't fit in with our values and priorities because we wouldn't be able to eat dinner together regularly. Obviously there will be times you won't be able to have dinner together, but we are really careful to protect that time as a family.[4]

The Joneses may not have time to gather around a meal as a family because it doesn't coordinate with their rigorous academic, social, and athletic calendar. But research shows that having a meal together as a family four times a week or more results in higher grades and decreased risk of depression or drug use. With each additional dinner, researchers found fewer emotional and behavioral problems, greater emotional well-being, and higher life satisfaction.[5]

Researchers also encourage parents to turn off all electronics (not just the TV, but phones and tablets too) while eating. As you can imagine, the quality of communication takes a nosedive when each family member is staring at a screen. Karol Ladd says,

> There's nothing that can take the place of eye-to-eye contact and just letting our kids see our eyes of love for them. A happy mom works toward communicating over the dinner table so her kids know she's listening. When we realize the hormones are going wild in our teenage kids, we need to listen a little bit more because during those times, they really want to be heard. As parents, we want to make sure the kids know our rules. If we could step back a little bit and just listen—not that we would change our rules—but the rules sure do go better when our kids know they've been heard.[6]

No need to replicate the fast-food, eat-in-the-car lifestyle of many modern families. Or those who dine at restaurants while engaging with screens more than each other. Your meals don't have to be homemade all the time. Gluten free, fat free, baked fresh, or reheated—it doesn't matter. What really matters is that your meals are served with love around the family table regularly. Be countercultural. Don't be in a hurry to leave the dinner table, and remember to turn off all your screens while eating.

The Return of Free Time

Dr. Gary Chapman has this reminder to slow down: "Life has to be balanced. Most of life is going to be scheduled, but there needs to be some time where you don't have to be doing anything. There's a place for getting a bucket of water and putting a stick in it and stirring it around."[7]

When you think of children worldwide, *play* is certainly a key characteristic of childhood. Through play, children learn how to get along with others, follow rules, develop interests and competencies, and experience joy. These are important building blocks to becoming an adult. Yet today's child is too busy to play with water in a bucket or make a fort out of cardboard boxes. He or she isn't allowed outside to play with neighbors for safety reasons. Children simply don't have the unstructured play that existed in the fifties.

One study from 1981 to 1997 revealed that children experienced a 25 percent decrease in play time and a 55 percent decrease in time talking with others at home.[8] Over this same period, anxiety, depression, feelings of helplessness, and narcissism in kids have continually increased.[9] A startling 85 percent of young people in recent samples have anxiety and depression scores greater than the average scores for the same age group in the fifties.[10]

Think about it. When you do something you enjoy with friends and have a good laugh, your mental health improves dramatically. Kids need that kind of free time to laugh and have fun without an adult micromanaging and directing every activity. There are plenty of opportunities for purposeful enrichment through education, sports, music, or clubs. What kids need more of these days is unstructured play. Not more screen time but free time. Downtime. The Joneses won't tell you this. They'll say you must be busy with lessons, appointments, games, and clubs to be well rounded. But the truly enlightened parent might just let their kids sit in the backyard for a long spell with just a bucket of water and a stick.

Wonderfully Made

As an only child, I never experienced sibling rivalry or the bonding of sisters. But I have a front-row seat to the interactions between my three kids. A few years ago, I was concerned my middle child, Noelle, might feel left out at times. Ethan is a high achiever; Lucy is the belle of the ball as the youngest. I got a story from the library about a middle child and had Noelle read it, and then I asked her a few questions. Turns out she loves being in the middle.

"I wouldn't want to be Ethan because he has too much responsibility," she said. "I don't want to be Lucy either. She's so young and she's not allowed to do a lot of things. I *love* being in the middle!" She still relishes her position in the birth order.

I love this example of being happy in your own spot. Not jockeying or wishing to be like someone else. Not coveting another's trophies, talents, or toys as the tenth commandment warns us about. You can enjoy being fearfully and wonderfully made, designed just as the Creator saw fit.

Fern Nichols talks about the joy of being a mother, regardless of the challenges your child may face:

> Let's say a mother has a special needs child. There is a happiness and joy knowing that when she ponders those verses in Psalm 139 that God knit every single little part of that child in the womb, there's a happiness in knowing God has a plan. That mom may say, "This is not my plan. But You created my child and everything You create is perfect. It is good. So You are going to get greater glory from this child's life in light of how You created him. You know the overall plan." That's happiness. It goes back to trusting the God you know.[11]

In today's Bible verse, it doesn't say, "Always give yourselves fully to keeping up with the Joneses." No, it says, "Always give yourselves fully to *the work of the Lord.*" When you do that, your life will not be in vain. Follow the priorities God gives you and you will find joy.

Today's Energy Boost

Find a window of time for your child to have free play today or tomorrow. More free play for your child will translate someday into more free time for you!

Today's Prayer

Lord, I want to give myself fully to Your work. Show me the unique things You are doing in my family and how I can join You and not fight against You. Give me wisdom to know what activities to continue and what activities to end. Help our family to have more uninterrupted meals together and free time to relax and play.

Yes to Being the Fun House

There, in the presence of the LORD your God, you and your
families shall eat and shall rejoice in everything you have put
your hand to, because the LORD your God has blessed you.

DEUTERONOMY 12:7

The beautifully wrapped box under the Christmas tree had my name on it. I wasn't surprised when I opened James's present—a spiffy black-and-pink pair of in-line skates. I knew he had ordered them with high hopes I would someday be able to glide down the boardwalk with him and the kids.

I received this gift with a smile *and* a grimace. Sure, I'd love to learn how to skate with my skater dude. James was the teen blading sensation in the eighties with a boom box on his shoulder. (I was the kid glued to the TV sitting on the couch.) I knew it would take determination, time, and a lot of ibuprofen and ice to use my Christmas gift.

So why in the world do I lace on those skates, put on a helmet, wrist guards, kneepads, and even the T-shirt of humiliation in underwear to pad my bottom? Two simple motivations: to make James happy through recreational companionship and to have fun with my kids.

The kids took to in-line skating much faster than I did (no surprise there). As they sit on a park bench waiting for me to catch up, they chant "Mommy! Mommy! Mommy!" and even in my embarrassment, I have to laugh. *This is fun*, I tell myself again and again. Yes, this is a lie, but someday I'm hoping it will be true. I'm going to fake it until I make it.

Having fun as a mom at times requires a bit of work, a dose of humility, and an ability to tap into your inner silly. I do out-of-my-comfort-zone, crazy things because I believe it's worth it to make fun memories together as a family. Things like skating, jujitsu, and camping come to mind. You don't have to be particularly good or skilled; you just have to be willing to show up for the party. And it helps if you don't take yourself too seriously.

My crazy, fun mom friend Hannah Keeley remembers her husband asking one evening, "Did you have fun today?" She thought about it and said, "No, I don't think I had fun today." Hannah says:

> We should go to bed every night and ask, "Did I have fun today?" It says in Psalm 35:27 that God takes joy in the prosperity of His servants. I think so many times we flip into this role of being this tyrannical mom. But if we can take time and have fun and understand one another…we have to open up our hearts and understand what makes our family members tick. Know the people you're partying with![12]

I think that's a great question to ask ourselves regularly: *Did I have fun today?* If it's been awhile since you could answer that question with a yes, hang on. We're going to talk about becoming the fun house in your neighborhood.

The Purpose-Driven Party Mom

Perhaps you've heard of *The Purpose-Driven Life* by Rick Warren. Guess what? Your party side can have purpose too. Before Karol Ladd became known through her books as the "Positive Lady," she was the "Party Lady." The first book she wrote when her kids were in preschool and kindergarten was *Parties with a Purpose*. It was about throwing fun, biblically themed parties to share God's love with others. As her girls, Joy and Grace, grew up, Karol wanted her home to be a fun house where her daughters and their friends would want to be.

> We didn't have a bunch of rules when kids came over. "No, you can't do that" and "No, you can't do that either" will make kids leave your house real quick. We had fun, simple games like sidewalk chalk. Kids would lie down and look at the clouds, play in the sprinklers, and make artwork at the kitchen table. We would host movie time with popcorn. We'd make tickets, use play money, and open up a concession stand. These things build memories and enjoyable experiences in the home.

During the high-school years, Karol wanted to have her girls' friends hang out at their house. So they always had fun food available, including a giant bowl of trail mix.

> Kids knew they were always welcome. The door would be open, and they could find a good snack. Kids could have lunch off campus, and during my daughter's senior year, I would walk into my kitchen and my daughter wouldn't even be there, but her friends would be. They knew our house was close and a happy place to be.[13]

When Ethan started kindergarten at an elementary school of more than a thousand students, we were looking for ways to connect with other families, beginning with Ethan's classroom. We decided to throw an ice-cream party. I printed out a simple invitation, cleared it with the teacher, and stuffed the student boxes with the invites. We held the party on the first Friday night of the school year. Everyone brought ice cream or toppings to share. The cost was minimal, and we had the opportunity to meet Ethan's future friends and their families. It was a big hit!

We've thrown that ice-cream party at the beginning of every school year since. It's been a wonderful tradition. We also host an annual class Christmas party where we sing Christmas carols to our neighbors and share the real story of Christmas from God's Word. The kids gather around the Christmas tree and listen while I read from Luke 2. Parents in the background listen too...and voilà, we have a party with purpose. For that one, we skip the ice cream and have families bring Christmas cookies to share instead. The peanut-butter cookies usually are to blame for my holiday weight gain, but I suppose I've already confessed my lack of control with cookies.

What's Your Thing?

As you've noticed, food is often connected to fun when it comes to kids, tweens, and teens (and moms). Dannah Gresh remembers always figuring out what kind of food her son Robby liked. In middle school, it was the "killer cookie"—an enormous hot chocolate-chip cookie smothered in ice cream and fudge. Food was a fun love language between Dannah and her son. She sought ways to connect with Robby from laser tag to speedboats. Dannah says,

It doesn't matter what your thing is. It just matters that there is a thing. You can be a sports mom and watch games together and wear matching jerseys. In middle school, our whole family played laser tag. I'm not a football girl, but put me in a laser-tag field and watch out! I'm going to hurt you!

During high school, we bought a broken-down speedboat. Going out in the boat was our thing. It's being intentional about finding those activities to connect. We have traditions we've done our whole life that the kids have grown up with. We get our Christmas tree on Black Friday every year. We make a big break-fast and go conquer the forest and cut down a tree. We always play "Grandma Got Run Over by a Reindeer" because we're classy like that. We're still doing this in their young adult years. It's our thing.[14]

So what's going to be your thing? What fun traditions and activities will you enjoy in your home? And what fun things will you do purely for yourself? Not everything has to be about dying to self, like me strapping on those skates of doom. James remembers his mom taking time for herself to pursue her hobbies and interests. She sailed, jogged, went out with friends, and participated in group Bible studies. James says,

I see moms who have no hobbies except for their kids. I'll ask, "What are your hobbies?" to which they reply, "I don't have hobbies. I have kids." Then I ask, "Well, if you had the time, what would your hobby be?" Then all of a sudden, they light up and get happy.

Anything carried to the extreme becomes an error. You have the dad who plays golf all weekend and never sees his family. I'm not talking about the extreme. I'm talking about having some fun hobbies outside of the kids. That's healthy for any mom.

So, my husband who pushes me to skates also gives me lots of space to rejuvenate myself with hobbies that please me. They tend to be much calmer and less risk-oriented. (Who ever got hurt reading a book or watching a movie?)

Get out your calendar and schedule in some fun. You'll be glad you did—and so will your kids!

A Word for Stepmoms from
Laura Petherbridge

The stepmom has to recognize the family has to create new traditions and memories. Don't get angry when the children draw upon their old memories of Christmas or summer vacation. Don't be jealous of that. Instead, work out some ways to create new memories that have fun things attached to them. Many things occur spontaneously. The things my stepsons and I laughed about were really nothing I planned or created. Try not to get so stressed out about every little thing. Stop trying to make everything a Norman Rockwell moment, especially during the holidays.

I desperately wanted my stepsons to have this idyllic wonderful holiday. I come from a big Italian family on my dad's side, and I tried this Norman Rockwell meets the Godfather moment in my home. They had no interest in any of that. If I were their biological mom, of course they would want that. But they have no family connection to me, so I had to learn not to be offended or hurt by that. Create new memories with your stepchildren that you will laugh about in the future. Twenty-eight years later, the things we laugh about are none of the things I thought we would laugh about and remember.[15]

Today's Energy Boost

Ask yourself: "Have I had fun today?" If the answer is no, it's not too late to change that. Maybe you can sit down to knit, take a walk around the block, play a game, watch a funny video, or do whatever it is you do for fun.

Today's Prayer

Lord, I want to overflow with joy. I don't want to just survive day by day as a mom. I want to have fun. I want my life of faith to be attractive to my children. I don't want to be sour, stressed, or ungrateful. Help me to rejoice in You and find many reasons to laugh today.

Day 29

Yes to Service

*"Just as the Son of Man did not come to be served, but
to serve, and to give his life as a ransom for many."*
MATTHEW 20:28

My friend Gwen Smith has been called to lead worship. Although she travels extensively to speak and sing, she also serves in her home church on the worship team. This involves some sacrifice, particularly at 6:20 on Sunday mornings when she has to leave her cozy home for practice. She goes with coffee. Gwen says:

> My family feels the sacrifice of it too. I think it's important to model—you are my family, you are my children, but you are not my world. My first priority is my Lord. Showing my kids service to the Lord and the church can be balanced with my service to them.[16]

If we want our kids to find fulfillment in serving Christ and others, we need to show them how it's done. That can be accomplished through serving joyfully in our local church, volunteering at school, going on short-term mission trips, or saving money to support a child in a faraway land.

Abraham Lincoln said, "To ease another's heartache is to forget one's own."[17] The happy mom realizes the path to joy is paved by doing good to others in the name of Christ. Living selfishly and accumulating more stuff doesn't bring joy. But serving others does. Perhaps we think we're shielding our kids by providing them a cushioned, carefree life devoid of menial service. Today's average child rarely has to stoop down to serve. We moms are the ones doing all the stooping. No wonder we're all so unhappy at times.

Life Outside the Walls

From their home in Texas, Kristen Welch and her family of five are making a big difference on the streets of Kenya through Mercy House, a home for pregnant girls.[18] Kristen has always been an intentional mom, but she remembers placing her focus on the *inside* of the walls of her home. Although they did many good faith-based things, a life-changing shift occurred when she began focusing on what their family could do *outside* those walls.

As a mommy blogger, Kristen was invited by Compassion International to blog about the slums of Nairobi, Kenya, by experiencing it first-hand. That trip began a chain of events and a string of yeses to God that led to the founding of Mercy House. Kristen knew how important it was to get the whole family on board. She remembers their first trip as a family to Kenya:

> I wanted to expose my kids to the world and I also wanted them to understand what we were sacrificing for. Why we were making the life choices we were making. I wanted them to hold a baby and understand the power of a yes.
>
> What ended up being really powerful for me as a mother was seeing broken families on the other side of the world look at our family and see a whole family for the first time. I'll never forget, my youngest had just turned four and she was completely comfortable after two weeks. She was disobeying me and being a normal kid. I took her aside and disciplined her, and the residents overheard me. I was embarrassed at first, but they loved it. They said, "We've never seen a mother discipline her child out of love." It was such a picture to them.
>
> Serving as a family has brought out really good things, but it's also brought out our humanity. It's not all nice and clean. It's work, and there are complaints and whining. "Why do we have to do this?" That's part of serving. I talk to moms who say, "Well, my kids complain." Welcome to the club! I complain too. It's hot or I'm tired, but that doesn't mean we don't serve. God uses that mess to bring Him glory. When we're saying yes to God, yes to eternal things that matter, there is a very satisfying soul-quenching thing that happens deep within us. It really spills over into our families and makes us different people.

Locally, Kristen's family works with refugees in their city. She remembers volunteering for a huge garage sale where they were so understaffed that her children ended up taking key roles. Her fourteen-year-old and twelve-year-old were in charge of large areas, and her seven-year-old assisted them. It was a ten-hour day, and Kristen remembers looking out over the parking lot at them and feeling guilty. On the way home, her kids thanked her and said it was the best day of their life.

It reminds me of this quote from coach John Wooden, "You can't live a perfect day without doing something for someone who will never be able to repay you."[19] Kristen says,

> When we can ignite a passion in our kids and expand their worldview and change their perspective of how other people live, we're giving them life lessons. My kids are still normal. They're not always champing at the bit to go serve someone, but they see the world differently. And that does make me very happy. We're all much more content. They are more grateful for what they have.
>
> I think we have to push away the requirements that our culture puts on everything—the supersized, big, mega, value meal. We always want bigger and better. The kingdom of God is upside down. It doesn't look like how the world looks. Jesus wants those small yeses. That's where we meet Him.[20]

Be the Sonshine

Opportunities to serve may take you halfway around the world or right down the street. For our family service project, we decided to concentrate on our kids' elementary school and starting an afterschool Bible club. An online search led us to Sonshine Haven, a nonprofit dedicated to instilling godly character and sustainable life skills to children through an afterschool program called Sonshine Club. We became their fortieth club. Every Friday school is in session, my family is there in the multipurpose room for one hour with sixty-five awesome (and noisy) kids from kindergarten through sixth grade.

We have a team of volunteers, including moms from the school and retired teachers from our church. We sing worship songs, run games, serve snacks, present a Bible lesson, and have small-group discussions. Does it take effort to serve? You bet—it's a huge weekly time commitment and a ton of details (picture me going through permission slips and typing out attendance sheets). Is it worth it? On so many levels, a resounding yes! My kids are learning how to invite their friends to Sonshine Club and to share God's love without embarrassment in a public school setting. They have several friends who attend, so we are getting to know our kids' friends and teaching them valuable truths from the Bible.

James and I serve together, which is a huge bonus. You know how difficult it can be to find a service project that both husband and wife find meaningful. Since we have three kids in the school, we'll be running Sonshine Club for a long time. Imagine the impact of a weekly ministry in the life of a student potentially from kindergarten all the way through sixth grade. Here's a note I received from one fourth-grade girl:

> *Dear Miss Arlene,*
>
> *Thank you for helping us learn about the Bible. I enjoy being here and will cherish it.*

And what's sweeter still? Our kids are learning to serve alongside us. They help with skits, prepare tickets, buy prizes with me (they like that part), and help clean up each week.

Before you put my family on a wobbly pedestal, please know there are several weeks I don't feel like putting on my turquoise Sonshine Club T-shirt and directing a relay race for sixty-five hyper kids. But I show up each week because it's on the calendar. We may begin a service project because something tugs on our heartstrings, but emotions fade, and then we've got to let the calendar boss our feelings around. Having a reoccurring family service project on the calendar is a powerful way to weave service into the fabric of our family.

There is no question in my mind that God directed us to be involved with Sonshine Club. We weren't directed to start a nonprofit in Kenya like Kristen's family. We were led to run an afterschool Bible club in our community. The point of today's reading is not to ask, "So, which will it be? Are you going to start an international nonprofit or Bible club now?" The question is, "What is one way God is calling *you* to serve?" As Kristen likes to say, your yes matters to God.

Chores Will Not Kill Your Child

Your child can also learn about service in the comfort of your own home by doing chores and helping you. Can I hear an amen? Chores build teamwork and fight that dreaded entitlement spirit prevalent in today's youth culture. Chores teach a good work ethic and build a child's competence and confidence. Researchers compared children who had daily chores and children who did not. Here's what they found:

> Children who performed household chores showed more compassion for their siblings and other family members than children who did not share in family responsibility. Even more interesting was the fact that not all chores are equal. The kids who did family-care chores like setting the table, feeding the cat, or bringing in firewood showed more concern for the welfare of others than children who had only self-care responsibilities, such as making their own bed and hanging up their own clothes.
>
> Such research validates the obvious. Whenever children participate in the care of others, they grow sensitive to human need. Include your children in the experience of serving others daily.[21]

Going to the ends of the earth to serve may very well begin with setting the dinner table and unloading the dishwasher. Start serving within the walls of your home, and before long, your family's heart for service will overflow to bless others on your street, city, and around the world.

Today's Energy Boost

This is the only action step in the book about shopping—which is an energy boost to many of you. Visit Kristen's website at MercyHouseKenya.org and shop the online store's global marketplace and check out Fair Trade Friday.

Today's Prayer

I know the Bible says the Son of Man did not come to be served, but to serve. Lord, help me to follow Your example of being a servant. Speak to me today about a specific way I can serve You this week. Help me notice service projects that might involve my children. Create a heart to serve within me and within the hearts of my kids.

Day 30

Yes to Mission Impossible

"'If you can?' said Jesus. "Everything is possible for one who believes."
Mark 9:23

Ethan sat in the shopping cart smiling while I sped around the store in utter panic. Would there be a blowout? I had a spare outfit, but what if I needed a towel to wipe up the mess? It was Ethan's first time in public without a diaper or pull-up. My toddler was wearing big boy underwear. I watched him constantly, looking for any sign of impending urination. I was a mess. Ethan on the other hand stayed clean and dry.

During that potty training stage, it felt like mission impossible to go out for stretches of time without a safety net. Going to the bathroom in the toilet is old hat now. Potty training seems like a small issue compared to middle school, raging hormones, and paying for college someday. Being a mom is kind of like being a secret agent who's constantly handed new impossible missions to accomplish. When one mission is complete, the next assignment is given.

Attitude plays a huge part in our success. As Noelle likes to tell me, "Mom, if you believe you can't do it, then you can't. But if you believe you can, then you can!" We can look at the odds stacked against us and throw in the towel. Or we can bravely forge ahead.

Here are a few seemingly impossible missions today that are possible with God's help. Let's be countercultural.

Raising Generous Kids in a Gimme World

Pastor and author Dave Stone writes in *How to Raise Selfless Kids in a Self-Centered World*, "When we live with an attitude of generosity, it can be a key aspect of our legacy and a characteristic that will show up again and again in the branches of our family tree."[22] When their church was in a building campaign several years ago, Dave's nine-year-old son, Sam, filled out a pledge card to give a whopping two hundred dollars—his entire allowance for two years. Dave writes:

> Every week he gave every penny of his income to the church. No spending money. No ice cream sundaes. About nine months into the commitment, I spoke at a father-and-son retreat in Texas, and Sam went with me. They asked if Sam would share for a few minutes about how, as a young boy, he was living for Christ. So Sam shared some thoughts and then did a Christian rap song he'd memorized. They liked the rap so much that they asked him to do it again on Sunday morning in all of their worship services—for about four thousand people. The following week Sam got a check in the mail—a love offering, if you will, in gratitude for what he had shared. Any guesses on the amount? Yep. Two hundred dollars to the penny.[23]

As your kids are exposed to your generosity, they will try out generosity themselves. God notices, and your child will truly learn it is more blessed to give than to receive.

Raising Bible-Strong Kids in a Biblically Illiterate World

According to the 2014 "The State of the Bible" report by the Barna Group and American Bible Society, 81 percent of US adults said they consider themselves highly, moderately, or somewhat knowledgeable about the Bible. Yet only 43 percent were able to name the first five books of the Bible.[24]

Kenneth Berding, professor of New Testament at my alma mater Biola University, says, "My own experience teaching a class of new college freshman every year for the past 15 years suggests to me that although students 15 years ago knew little about the Bible upon entering my classes, today's students on average know even less about the Bible." For example, one of his students did not know that Saul in the New Testament was different than King Saul in the Old Testament.[25]

Here are a few ideas to raise kids who know and treasure the Word of God:

- Read a Bible story at bedtime to your young children every night. As your kids get older, this nighttime ritual will morph into them reading the Bible on their own.

- Create a doable Bible reading plan starting in upper elementary school.

- Set goals such as "Read the New Testament before sixth-grade graduation." Have a family party when goals are met.

- Memorize Bible verses together. Have quiz shows complete with dollar earnings—sibling versus sibling and child versus parent.

- Sing songs with Scripture in them. Some of my favorite artists are Seeds Family Worship and the Go Fish Guys.[26]

- Let your children catch you reading your Bible often.

Raising Academic Kids in an ADHD World

You remember my friend Dr. Jennifer Degler who sat in tears surrounded by a huge stack of books after she learned about her son Jake's ADHD diagnosis. Students in her state are not tested for learning disabilities until second grade. Jennifer knew the ground her son would lose by waiting, so she paid out of pocket to have him tested in kindergarten. The test showed Jake was at high risk for complete reading failure. Instead of accepting that prediction, Jennifer's family saved and lived frugally so Jake could go to a reading center and work with a tutor three times a week. Jennifer remembers the Lord using John 9 and the story of the man born blind.

> His disciples asked him, "Rabbi, who sinned, this man or his parents, that he was born blind?"
>
> "Neither this man nor his parents sinned," said Jesus, "but this happened so that the works of God might be displayed in him" (John 9:2-3).

Jennifer said, "I was trying to figure out what did I do to make Jake like this? It's one of the few times in my life when I've really almost felt the Lord directly saying to me, 'Jennifer, you will see me glorified through what I'm going to do in Jake.'"

At some point when Jake was in fifth grade, Jennifer heard him reading out loud from the other room. She started crying because she didn't know he could read that well. At fifth-grade graduation, Jake's teacher gave him the student-of-the-year award. Jake was on the principal's list for making As and Bs. Jennifer wanted to stand on the chair and shout, "Who has seen the glory of the Lord? I have seen the glory of the Lord!" But she knew that would be embarrassing.

By sixth grade, Jake tested into the advanced math class. By the end of eighth grade, the school tested him again and he didn't qualify for learning disorders anymore. By eleventh grade, he took AP US history and got a C his first semester and a B his second.[27]

Don't give up. Keep investing in reading and tutoring for your child. You will eventually see results that will make you want to shout too.

Raising Christ Followers in a Prodigal World

After graduating from high school, many young adults stop going to church and question the beliefs of their childhood. According to a Barna study, 61 percent of twentysomethings who have been churched at one point in their teen years are now spiritually disengaged (not actively attending church, reading the Bible, or praying).[28] As parents, we must keep praying and keep believing for any prodigals to come home.

When Janet Thompson was raising her daughter as a single mom, she remembers:

> I was successful by the world's standards. I did well financially, but while I was raising her in those formative years, I was backsliding and she became like me. When she was sixteen, I returned to my senses and rededicated my life to Christ at a Harvest Crusade. I thought my daughter would make a U-turn like I did. But she didn't want anything to do with it. She thought I was weird and a freak. She took off to college to live with her boyfriend and that broke my heart.

> Down on my knees, I cried, "Lord I've tried everything." I began praying Scripture every single day for six years. My daughter was insulted at first that I thought she needed prayer. But six years later, she started to make some changes. She dated a non-Christian and they got engaged. We gave them a biblically based premarital course, and they both got saved! We baptized them two weeks

before the wedding. It was beyond my wildest dreams. Now we speak together and people ask my daughter, "How do you feel about your mom calling you a prodigal?" To which she replies, "Well, I was one!"[29]

God is faithful and He chases down prodigals regularly—even right before they walk down the aisle. God is never intimidated by the impossible. Today's verse from Mark 9:23 is Jesus's response to a father's plea for his demon-possessed son to be healed. What could be a more impossible challenge for a parent? Listen to the exchange between a desperate father and Jesus in Mark 9:22-24:

> "If you can do anything, take pity on us and help us." "'If you can'?" said Jesus. "Everything is possible for one who believes." Immediately the boy's father exclaimed, "I do believe; help me overcome my unbelief"!

Let's cry out like this father. Whether your impossible mission right now is potty training, getting your child to sleep through the night, or dealing with pornography on a smartphone, know that your heavenly Father sees you. He will equip you to do the impossible. Your mission as a mom will be a success as you follow your commander, Jesus Christ.

Today's Energy Boost

Time for a quick attitude check. Circle the phrases you say more often to yourself:

I can…

I can't…

I believe…

I don't believe…

Today's Prayer

Lord, I surrender my impossible missions to You. You know what is happening in the hearts of my children today. Take my concerns as a mom and give me courage to face challenges with faith. I do believe in You; help my unbelief. Keep me on task, on mission, to raise kids who love You and keep Your commands. May our family be a light for You.

Day 31

Yes to the Empty Nest

Children are a heritage from the LORD,
offspring a reward from him.
Like arrows in the hands of a warrior
are children born in one's youth.

PSALM 127:3-4

When my friend Nikki was pregnant with her first (a boy), she attended the wedding of her husband's coworker. She didn't even know the couple, yet she cried through the whole thing. Her husband asked her what was wrong. She said she realized one day *she* would be the mom giving away her son in marriage. She longed to comfort the mother of the groom and tell her she understood what she was going through.

Without a doubt, we moms are intricately attached to our children (even before they're born!). But God never designed us to be *permanently* attached. Children are like arrows. They are meant to be shot out into the world, to be useful, not to be kept in the quiver of our homes, living with mom and dad throughout young adulthood. To be a happy mom, we have to make peace with that future empty nest.

I remember going to an event with my mentor, Pam Farrel. On the way, she asked if we could quickly stop by a friend's house because it was right on the way. As we sat chatting in her friend's living room, I couldn't get over the house. It was neat, spacious, and recently vacuumed. But what struck me most was that it was quiet. All her children were grown and gone. I'm sure the house was quite noisy in its heyday. The photos of her children that lined the walls and bookshelves attested to that. *Someday my home will be this quiet,* I thought. *All I will have are pictures in the house.*

Some of you, like my friend Nikki, will want to grab a tissue about now. Others of you want to fast forward to that day of freedom. No matter where you are on the continuum, that empty nest is coming.

A few months ago, Lucy was learning how to ride a bicycle. I was walking behind her bike and giving her instructions. "You're too close to the curb. Slow down. Go around the speed bump. Watch out!" Sick of my constant stream of orders, she said in exasperation, "You are making me under control!"

So I stopped giving orders. And guess what happened? Lucy took off on her bicycle. Completely on her own. I couldn't keep up with her. When I was finally quiet, she began to fly. If we keep our children "under control" when we ought to be slowly letting go, it can make them feel out of control. Our hovering holds them back.

My friend Gwen Smith remembers the first time her kids took off in a car—all by themselves.

> Yesterday they went to youth group and volleyball by themselves, and I was like yay! I don't have to take them anymore because I've been a major taxi driver for seventeen years. But there's also a component of, *Oh, there goes my heart*. It's a whole new level of trusting God. That's what I'm finding out about the teen years. It is release after release.[30]

College Bound

It was a little scary to think about the empty nest for Karol Ladd. She wondered what it would be like with both her daughters out of the house. She thought about how much she would miss them:

> You think, *Who am I without them?* Our identity sometimes gets wrapped up in being a mom and raising our kids. Entering the empty-nest stage was a big transition but a good one. It meant my girls were flying on their own. They were becoming who God meant for them to be.
>
> I remember the very day Joy left for college. My husband and I came back to the house. We smiled, kissed, and said, "It's just us!" I would say this to any wife and mom—it's so important to

maintain a strong relationship with your husband because before you know it, when that empty nest arrives, it's just you for a while.

Although we say empty nest, we still are pouring into our kids. When they go off to college, they still need a mom. They still need me in a different way. They call me up, crying or sharing what's going on. They still need advice—and care packages. I think possibly one of the most important words for a happy mom is to be *flexible* and to recognize each stage only lasts momentarily. Be happy with each stage. Enjoy and embrace each stage of your child's life—even the empty nest.[31]

Marci Seither, mother of six, had babies in three decades, beginning in the eighties. Marci writes in *Empty Nest: Strategies to Help Your Kids Take Flight* about a trip she took with her friends. She discovered she was one of only a few who weren't on some form of antidepressant.

The biggest question they had for me was, "How do you cope?" I thought back to the generations where neighbors knew each other and women met together to learn basics of canning and sewing. They also supported each other during transitional times. The sense of community was strong because we weren't flooded by artificial socializing. One real friend is much better than a hundred virtual friends. We can be connected via the worldwide web, yet our level of loneliness is rising.

When our kids leave home and our routine becomes very different, it is important to expand yourself outside of the box and make new friends, pursue new interests, and reconnect with people who care about you.[32]

Dealing with the often difficult transition to empty nest begins with finding a friend who gets it. Your young adult children won't be the only ones making new social connections when they leave the house. You will be too.

Rich Mom, Poor Mom

Our culture equates being rich with material possessions. Yet being a rich mom has very little to do with our bank account, and a whole lot to do with legacy. The apostle Paul attributed Timothy's spiritual maturity to his grandmother Lois and his mother, Eunice (2 Timothy 1:5). Without a believing father present, Timothy's rich spiritual heritage was passed to him by his mother and grandmother. Janet Thompson comments:

> What a legacy—your honest, rich faith handed down. It can't get much better than being able to say you passed down a love for Jesus to your children and grandchildren. You don't know how much time you have to leave a legacy. Those of us who become grandparents are privileged to have that time.
>
> It's such a joy to be a mom. Younger moms may think, *I'm going to be a mom until my kids get married.* But I learned that it never stops. You never stop being a parent. It's just the way you parent that changes. You still have a relevant part in their life, not criticizing but encouraging in ways that will help. It's an eye-opener when grandkids come along; another whole generation to be praying for and to have in your life. That's what God's plan was for us. We never retire from motherhood.[33]

The poor mom is a mom who neglects to pass along faith in Christ to her children. We read in Psalm 78:5-7:

> He decreed statutes for Jacob
>   and established the law in Israel,
> which he commanded our ancestors
>   to teach their children,
> so the next generation would know them,
>   even the children yet to be born,
>   and they in turn would tell their children.
> *Then* they would put their trust in God
>   and would not forget his deeds
>   but would keep his commands.

Read the passage again, now placing your emphasis and attention on that tiny italicized word *then.* Don't miss the aha moment. When do your children place their trust in God? After *you* have told them and modeled obedience in front of them. Your children will know God's commands from your teaching. Don't remain silent about spiritual things. While your children are under your roof, constantly talk about the commandments and character of God, and the wondrous things God has done in your life.

When the time comes for your child to fly away, he or she will be ready to soar for God and pass on faith to the next generation.

When Lucy was four years old, she observed a blackbird sitting on our fence, and then it flew away. "Usually when they get on the fence, they are getting ready to fly away," she said sentimentally.

Our children are designed by their Creator to fly away. When they're sitting on the fence, peering out into the wide, big world, and leaning forward, we know they're getting ready to soar. The same little children who say, "Mommy, I want to stay with you forever!" will someday pack up their belongings and leave our nest.

Noelle loves to shower me with kisses and hugs whether I'm just leaving for the grocery store or saying goodnight. "I don't ever want to let go!" she'll exclaim. It's inevitable that one day Noelle will let go, but I can always hold on to her in my heart. After all, I'll always be her mother.

Today's Energy Boost

If you're feeling a bit suffocated by your kids, or one of them is pushing your buttons today, remember the little blackbird sitting on the fence. Someday your children will be gone from your nest. Get perspective and enjoy them today.

Today's Prayer

Your Word says children are a heritage from You. Thank You for the rich treasure of my children. I release my kids to You. I know ultimately they will become adults, and it's my prayer they will follow You all the days of their lives. May they experience abundant life and joy today. And may we all dwell in Your house forever.

Conclusion

Be a Smiley

We were waiting to board a long flight from Baltimore to San Diego, and I noticed a mom who looked like actress Jennifer Garner, except with red hair. She was wearing a baby in a sling and holding hands with a toddler. Her baby cried like everyone else's at the gate, but there was something very odd about this mom. She was happy. She was easygoing and smiled broadly at other passengers. Was she not aware that she should be stressed out of her mind traveling with two girls under two years old? Other moms were shushing their kids, chasing their toddlers, and bouncing babies up and down nervously. That's certainly what I looked like when my kids were that age.

Granted, that happy mom may have been born with a sunnier disposition than most and be totally chill in her personality. But I venture to say that many days, she chooses to smile. She makes a conscious effort not to freak out, but to simply enjoy the moments to the best of her ability… including cross-country flights.

My family of five took up two rows in the airplane near this happy mom. About three hours into the trip, one of the flight attendants leaned over and asked how we were doing. "Treasure these days," she said to me with a smile. "You'll snap your fingers and they are over. My girls are twenty-seven and twenty-eight and they live halfway across the country."

Treasure these days. You've heard that advice too, haven't you? When you keep this perspective, being a mother becomes more of a joy and less of a chore. The cross-country flights aren't so bad when you remember that in a matter of time, you'll be traveling not *with* your kids but to *visit* your kids.

I have the joy of living in the same city as my parents, so I get to visit them often. My mom is the happiest lady you'll ever meet. I'm sedate in comparison. She laughs her way through problems and will greet you as if she's known you for years.

I asked if she had any words of advice. Lean in, this is the Yoda of happiness speaking now. She said,

> God gave us free will, and we can choose what to do when faced with a difficult situation that is not our choice. It's easy to be happy when things are going our way. Each morning, we choose what we will wear. In the same way, we also choose what attitude we will have for the day. Trials will hit us in life. We can choose to be revengeful, angry, or hopeless. We can feel unloved and uncared for. But I stubbornly choose to believe God loves me and cares about what happens to me. That helps me cope in a positive way with whatever situation I am faced with. It's impossible to be happy without knowing and believing that God loves us and is in control. That's what keeps me smiling!

There's one word my mom repeated again and again. Do you see it? *Choose.* When you boil it down, it's your choice to become a happy mom or an unhappy mom. Even my mom, who seemed to bounce right out of the womb grinning, has to *choose*. Don't pin the blame on difficult children or circumstances. The choice to move forward with a smile on your face is yours and yours alone. The good news is you don't walk alone. The other word my mom repeats is *God*. He loves you and will never leave or forsake you.

Hot Plates and Toasty Fingers

I was frying eggs one morning for the family. (Yes, my eggs are about as good as my cookies.) I set plates on the stovetop next to the pan, thinking that would expedite the serving and keep the eggs hot. They were hot all right. So much so that when Noelle grabbed her plate with both hands, she burned her fingers. Poor Noelle was such a trooper. She didn't even drop the hot plate—she handed it off to James who dropped it quickly in the sink. Noelle started to cry from the pain as I got ice for her fingers. I felt like a terrible mom. But she wasn't mad at all. She knew it was an accident.

Moms, we will do things on accident that will hurt our children. When that happens, apologize, ask for forgiveness, and move on. Don't walk around soaked in guilt for doing something you didn't mean to do. As I tell Lucy when she groans and grunts when she misprints a word, just erase your mistake and try again.

After the hot plate and toasty fingers incident, I was chatting with Ethan. I asked, "Would you rather be the one who caused the pain or the one who had the pain?" He answered, "The one who had the pain." I wholeheartedly agree. It's a horrible feeling to be the one responsible for someone's pain, especially a loved one. With this in mind, let's choose each day to bless, not curse, our children. And when your children hurt you from time to time with their words or actions, take heart. Better to be wronged than to be the wrongdoer.

Accidents and missteps happen in every family. But that's not where the focus should be. The happy mom fixes her eyes on success. I heard the following while listening to David Jeremiah's *Turning Point* radio program:

> Sometimes we get the idea because it is so abused that God is not interested in us succeeding. I even hear sometimes from coaches who are Christians the idea is sort of like this: "We learn as much from losing as we do from winning. In fact, sometimes it's good to lose so we can build character." Well, I don't buy that for a minute. I've discovered in my own life that I need to try as hard as I can to win because I'm going to lose enough whether I want to or not. Isn't that true? And when the losing comes, it's going to teach me what I need to learn. I don't need to try to lose, it's automatic. But I need to work hard at winning.[1]

Moms, we need to work hard at winning. For the past thirty-one days, we've been focusing on five keys to becoming a happy mom. Which of these keys have resonated with you the most?

H = Becoming *Healthy*

A = Becoming *Action-Oriented*

P = Becoming *Prayerful*

P = Becoming *Perseverant*

Y = Becoming *Yes-Filled*

The impact of reading this book can last much longer than one month in your mom life. By regularly taking stock of what's going on in your heart, you can make necessary adjustments to boost your personal happiness. When you get the blues or feel your blood pressure rising, go through this quick checklist:

- Are you taking care of yourself physically?
- Are you using Alpha Speech (see Day 8), acting like the leader of your children?
- Have you prayed about your kids today?
- Have you laughed today?
- Are you doing things for your kids they should be doing themselves?

Having regular times of self-evaluation and resetting your attitude will help you win more and more as a mom. Don't dwell on what you don't have. Dwell on what you do have. You have at your disposal everything you need to become a happy mom.

Home Is Where Your Story Begins

Kendra Smiley grew up in a "pretty upsetting" home, as she calls it. Her dad was a good provider but an alcoholic. Her mom was unloved. Kendra didn't know Jesus then. Although Kendra wasn't raised in a happy home, her story didn't end there.

> I bought a big plaque and put it in the foyer of my home. It reads "Home is where your story begins." When you have had a rough beginning, you can rewrite a new story for your family. My husband lets me be goofy, childlike, and fun. It's never too late to have a happy childhood.[2]

What a wonderful perspective. Even if you didn't have a happy home to draw from, you can create one for your children (and yourself). Kendra became a "Smiley" by marriage. Allow me to grant you permission to become a "smiley" by choice.

When I was pregnant with Ethan, I remember being in church on Mother's Day with my baby bump. I was beyond happy to finally be among the ones standing as mothers. Even though my baby was yet to be born, the church was kind enough to give me my first Mother's Day gift. It was a white mug dated Mother's Day 2004 with this verse: "Every wise woman builds her house" (Proverbs 14:1 HCSB).

Do you remember that wonder and awe you felt when you first held your newborn? No doubt you smiled at your precious bundle, just like I smiled at my seven-pound lump. Don't stop smiling now that your baby is a hyperactive boy or a moody teen girl. *Every wise woman builds her house.* Your joy will carry your child through to adulthood, building a home story that will be worth telling and repeating.

Notes

Introduction: Ditch the Crowd

1. www.brainyquote.com/quotes/quotes/e/ermabombec164138.html (accessed February 4, 2015).
2. "Tired and Stressed, but Satisfied: Moms Juggle Kids, Career and Identity," *Barna Group*, May 6, 2014, www.barna.org/barna-update/family-kids/669-tired-stressed-but-satisfied-moms-juggle-kids-career-identity#.VOy_4mBMvGg (accessed February 22, 2015).
3. To learn more about *The Compound Effect: Jumpstart Your Income, Your Life, Your Success* by Darren Hardy, visit http://thecompoundeffect.com/.
4. Personal interview with Rhonda Rhea, August 14, 2014.
5. Personal interview with Karol Ladd, August 14, 2014.

Key 1: Becoming Healthy

1. Carol Dweck, *Mindset: The New Psychology of Success* (New York: Ballantine Books, 2006).
2. Coach John Wooden with Steve Jamison, *Wooden: A Lifetime of Observations and Reflections On and Off the Court* (Chicago, IL: Contemporary Books, 1997), 68.
3. Personal interview with Kendra Smiley, August 5, 2014.
4. Personal interview with Hannah Keeley, August 13, 2014.
5. www.brainyquote.com/quotes/authors/e/erma_bombeck_3.html (accessed January 13, 2015).
6. Regent University chapel with Zig Ziglar, Spring 1998.
7. Olga Khazan, "For Depression, Prescribing Exercise Before Medication," *Atlantic*, March 24, 2014, www.theatlantic.com/health/archive/2014/03/for-depression-prescribing-exercise-before-medication/284587/ (accessed February 19, 2015).
8. Ayren Jackson-Cannady, "Sweat: 7 Reasons It Does a Body Good," *Fitness*, www.fitnessmagazine.com/health/sweat-health-benefits/ (accessed January 19, 2015).
9. "Physical Activity Guidelines for Americans," www.health.gov/paguidelines/guidelines/ (accessed January 19, 2015).
10. www.jacklalanne.com/index.php?select=LaLanneisms (accessed February 19, 2015).
11. Personal interview with Pam Farrel, March 5, 2013.
12. Interview with Kendra Smiley.
13. Ali Mohamadi, "Does Losing Sleep Mean Gaining Weight?," *ABC News*, December 6, 2004, http://abcnews.go.com/Health/story?id=305906 (accessed February 20, 2015).
14. "Insomnia," National Sleep Foundation, http://sleepfoundation.org/sleep-disorders-problems/insomnia (accessed December 27, 2014).
15. Personal interview with Gwen Smith, August 24, 2014.
16. Personal interview with Fern Nichols, August 13, 2014.

17. www.brainyquote.com/quotes/quotes/b/benjaminfr165455.html (accessed February 20, 2015).

18. David Jeremiah, *What Are You Afraid Of?* (Carol Stream, IL: Tyndale House Publishers, 2013), xiv.

19. Interview with Karol Ladd.

20. *Focus on the Family* broadcast, "Helping Your Family Thrive Spiritually (Part 1)," airdate August 20, 2014, www.focusonthefamily.com/media/focus-on-the-family-daily-international/helping-your-family-thrive-spiritually-pt1 (accessed August 27, 2014).

21. Interview with Karol Ladd.

22. Interview with Laura Petherbridge.

23. www.quotationspage.com/quote/2673.html (accessed January 20, 2015).

24. www.churchleaders.com/outreach-missions/outreach-missions-blogs/156530-scott_wil liams_10_spiritual_tonics.html (accessed December 10, 2014).

25. Personal interview with Dr. Jennifer Degler, November 17, 2014.

26. Jay Payleitner, *52 Things Husbands Need from Their Wives* (Eugene, OR: Harvest House Publishers, 2013), 96.

Key 2: Becoming Action-Oriented

1. Personal interview with Dannah Gresh, September 9, 2014.

2. Dr. Kevin Leman, *Making Children Mind Without Losing Yours* (Grand Rapids, MI: Revell, a division of Baker Books, 2007), 20-21.

3. Interview with Gwen Smith.

4. Interview with Dannah Gresh.

5. Dannah Gresh, *Six Ways to Keep the "Good" in Your Boy* (Eugene, OR: Harvest House Publishers, 2012), 71.

6. Interview with Gwen Smith.

7. John Rosemond, Family Conference 2015, El Cajon, CA, February 21, 2015.

8. Quoted in Judith Newman, "Inside the Teenage Brain," *Parade*, November 28, 2010, http://parade.com/37715/parade/28-inside-the-teenage-brain (accessed January 12, 2015).

9. Personal interview with Janet Thompson, August 25, 2014.

10. Interview with Rhonda Rhea.

11. Personal interview with Kristen Welch, August 12, 2014.

12. Interview with Rhonda Rhea.

13. To see a video of Lucy facing her veggie medley, visit arlenepellicane.com and click on Family Album under Videos.

14. "What Is the Broken Windows Theory," *wiseGEEK*, www.wisegeek.com/what-is-the-broken-windows-theory.htm (accessed January 16, 2015).

15. Matthew Henry, *Matthew Henry's Commentary on the Whole Bible* (Peabody, MA: Hendrickson, 1994), 997.

16. Interview with Kendra Smiley.

17. Interview with Hannah Keeley.

18. Interview with Laura Petherbridge.

19. Interview with Hannah Keeley.

20. Philip Yancey, "Guilt Good and Bad," *Christianity Today*, November 18, 2002, www.christianitytoday.com/ct/2002/november18/36.112.html (accessed January 17, 2015).

21. Personal interview with Kathi Lipp, August 12, 2014.

22. Personal interview with Karen Ehman, January 13, 2015.

23. "Generation M²," Kaiser Family Foundation, January 20, 2010, http://kff.org/other/event/generation-m2-media-in-the-lives-of/ (accessed January 18, 2015).

24. "Too Much 'Screen Time' for Kids Could Cause Long-term Brain Damage, Warn Experts," *Huffington Post*, May 22, 2012, www.huffingtonpost.co.uk/2012/05/21/parenting-tv-time-bad-health-children_n_1533244.html (accessed January 18, 2015).

25. Interview with Dannah Gresh.

26. Interview with Hannah Keeley.

27. Interview with Kristen Welch.

28. Interview with Jennifer Degler.

29. Beth Kassab, "Are You Addicted to Your Smartphone?" *Orlando Sentinel*, November 25, 2013, http://articles.orlandosentinel.com (accessed February 10, 2015).

30. www.brainyquote.com/quotes/quotes/f/francoisde151040.html (accessed January 20, 2015).

31. To go deeper on this topic, read Arlene's book coauthored with Gary Chapman, *Growing Up Social: Raising Relational Kids in a Screen-Driven World* (Chicago: Northfield Publishing, 2014).

32. Interview with Dannah Gresh.

33. Interview with Kathi Lipp.

34. Interview with Janet Thompson.

35. For more information about *The Five Love Languages* by Dr. Gary Chapman, visit www.5lovelanguages.com

Key 3: Becoming Prayerful

1. Interview with Kathi Lipp.

2. Mary Meeker, "Internet Trends Report," All Things D, May 2013, http://allthingsd.com/20130529/mary-meekers-Internet-trends-report-is-back-at-d11-slides/. (accessed February 22, 2015).

3. "Nomophobia, the Fear of Not Having a Mobile Phone, Hits Record Numbers," June 2, 2013, www.news.com.au/technology/nomophobia-the-fear-of-not-having-a-mobile-phone-hits-record-numbers/story-e6frfro0-1226655033189 (accessed February 2, 2015).

4. Jun Young and David Kinnaman, *The Hyperlinked Life: Live with Wisdom in an Age of Information Overload* (Grand Rapids, MI: Zondervan, 2013), 24.

5. Susan Strife and Liam Downey, "Childhood Development and Access to Nature," National Center for Biotechnology Information, www.ncbi.nlm.nih.gov/pmc/articles/PMC3162362/ (accessed February 22, 2015).

6. Young and Kinnaman, *The Hyperlinked Life*, 57.

7. Stormie Omartian, *The Power of a Praying Parent* (Eugene, OR: Harvest House Publishers, 2014), 17-18.

8. To learn more about Moms in Prayer, visit www.momsinprayer.org.

9. Interview with Fern Nichols.

10. Interview with Rhonda Rhea.

11. www.thefreedictionary.com/haywire (accessed December 10, 2014).

12. Kathi Lipp, *I Need Some Help Here! Hope for When Your Kids Don't Go According to Plan* (Grand Rapids, MI: Revell, 2014), 19,28.

13. Interview with Karen Ehman.

14. Interview with Laura Petherbridge.

15. Interview with Karen Ehman.

16. Interview with Fern Nichols.

17. Interview with Dannah Gresh.

18. Interview with Karol Ladd.

19. Bill and Pam Farrel, *The 10 Best Decisions Every Parent Can Make* (Eugene, OR: Harvest House Publishers, 2006), 137,138.

Key 4: Becoming Perseverant

1. Interview with Kathi Lipp.

2. Dale Carnegie, *How to Win Friends and Influence People* (New York, NY: Pocket Books, a division of Simon & Schuster, 1982), 234.

3. Interview with Karen Ehman.

4. Interview with Dannah Gresh.

5. www.goodreads.com/quotes/1321824-today-is-mine-tomorrow-is-none-of-my-business-if (accessed February 3, 2015).

6. Interview with Dr. Jennifer Degler.

7. John Rosemond, *The Well-Behaved Child: Discipline That Really Works* (Nashville, TN: Thomas Nelson Publishers, 2009), 28.

8. Interview with Rhonda Rhea.

9. Karen Ehman, *Keep It Shut: What to Say, How to Say It, and When to Say Nothing at All* (Grand Rapids, MI: Zondervan, 2015), 92-93.

10. Interview with Laura Petherbridge.

11. https://books.google.com/books?isbn=0310338085 (accessed February 4, 2015).

12. Interview with Fern Nichols.

13. S. S. Buzzell, "Proverbs," in *The Bible Knowledge Commentary: An Exposition of the Scriptures,* ed. John F. Walvoord and Roy B. Zuck (Wheaton, IL: Victor Books, 1983).

14. "Study Shows 70 Percent of Americans Take Prescription Drugs," *CBS News,* June 20, 2013, www.cbsnews.com/news/study-shows-70-percent-of-americans-take-prescription-drugs/ (accessed February 6, 2015).

15. Interview with Kendra Smiley.

16. Interview with Rhonda Rhea.

17. Interview with Kristen Welch.

18. Rosemond, *The Well-Behaved Child,* 30.

19. "The Wizard's Wisdom: 'Woodenisms,'" *ESPN,* June 4, 2010, http://sports.espn.go.com/ncb/news/story?id=5249709 (accessed February 3, 2015).

20. Kristen Welch, "A Promise to My Teenagers," *We Are THAT Family* (blog), October 29, 2014, http://wearethatfamily.com/2014/10/a-promise-to-my-teenagers/ (accessed February 10, 2015). Used by permission.

21. Personal interview with John Rosemond, January 30, 2015.

22. www.brainyquote.com/quotes/authors/e/erma_bombeck.html (accessed January 28, 2014).

23. Interview with Rhonda Rhea.

24. Interview with Gwen Smith.

Key 5: Becoming Yes-Filled

1. Interview with John Rosemond.
2. www.brainyquote.com/quotes/quotes/e/ermabombec136498.html (accessed February 1, 2015).
3. Interview with Karen Ehman.
4. Personal interview with Ruth Schwenk, January 30, 2015.
5. Sharon Jayson, "Each Family Dinner Adds Up to Benefits for Adolescents," *USA Today*, March 24, 2013, www.usatoday.com/story/news/nation/2013/03/24/family-dinner-adolescent-bene fits/2010731/ (accessed February 16, 2015).
6. Interview with Karol Ladd.
7. Personal interview with Dr. Gary Chapman, August 14, 2013.
8. Scott Dannemiller, "The One Question Every Parent Should Quit Asking," *HuffPost Parents* (blog), January 20, 2015, www.huffingtonpost.com/scott-dannemiller/the-one-question-every-parent-should-quit-asking_b_6182248.html (accessed February 16, 2015).
9. Peter Gray, "The Decline of Play and the Rise of Psychopathology in Children and Adolescents," *American Journal of Play* (Spring 2011), www.psychologytoday.com/files/attachments/1195/ajp-decline-play-published.pdf (accessed February 16, 2015).
10. Ibid.
11. Interview with Fern Nichols.
12. Interview with Hannah Keeley.
13. Interview with Karol Ladd.
14. Interview with Dannah Gresh.
15. Interview with Laura Petherbridge.
16. Interview with Gwen Smith.
17. www.goodreads.com/quotes/tag/volunteerism (accessed February 3, 2015).
18. To learn more about Mercy House, visit www.mercyhousekenya.org.
19. www.brainyquote.com/quotes/quotes/j/johnwooden106293.html (accessed February 19, 2015).
20. 129 Interview with Kristen Welch.
21. Gary and Anne Marie Ezzo, *Growing Kids God's Way*, 5th ed. (Simi Valley, CA: Biblical Ethics for Parenting, 1999), 135.
22. Dave Stone, *How to Raise Selfless Kids in a Self-Centered World* (Nashville, TN: Thomas Nelson Publishers, 2012), 81.
23. Ibid., 80-81.
24. Lillian Kwon, "Biblical Illiteracy in US at Crisis Point, Says Bible Expert," *Christian Post*, June 16, 2014, www.christianpost.com/news/biblical-illiteracy-in-us-at-crisis-point-says-bible-expert-121626/ (accessed February 4, 2015).
25. Ibid.
26. To learn more about Seeds Family Worship and Go Fish Resources, visit www.seedsfamilyworship.com and www.gofishguys.com.
27. Interview with Dr. Jennifer Degler.
28. "Most Twentysomethings Put Christianity on the Shelf Following Spiritually Active Teen Years," Barna Group, www.barna.org/barna-update/article/16-teensnext-gen/147-most-twenty-some things-put-christianity-on-the-shelf-following-spiritually-active-teen-years#.VOTc92BMvGg (accessed February 16, 2015).
29. Interview with Janet Thompson.
30. Interview with Gwen Smith.

31. Interview with Karol Ladd.

32. Marci Seither, *Empty Nest: Strategies to Help Your Kids Take Flight* (Kansas City, MO: Beacon Hill Press, 2014), 145-46.

33. Interview with Janet Thompson.

Conclusion: Be a Smiley

1. David Jeremiah, "The Life of Joseph," *Turning Point*, airdate October 29, 2014, www.davidjeremiah.org/site/radio_archives.aspx (accessed October 29, 2014).

2. Interview with Kendra Smiley.

Bible Verses for the Happy Mom

These commandments that I give you today are to be on your hearts. Impress them on your children. Talk about them when you sit at home and when you walk along the road, when you lie down and when you get up (Deuteronomy 6:6-7).

Fix these words of mine in your hearts and minds; tie them as symbols on your hands and bind them on your foreheads. Teach them to your children, talking about them when you sit at home and when you walk along the road, when you lie down and when you get up (Deuteronomy 11:18-19).

This day I call the heavens and the earth as witnesses against you that I have set before you life and death, blessings and curses. Now choose life, so that you and your children may live and that you may love the LORD your God, listen to his voice, and hold fast to him (Deuteronomy 30:19-20).

Arise, cry out in the night,
   as the watches of the night begin;
pour out your heart like water
   in the presence of the Lord.
Lift up your hands to him
   for the lives of your children.
                       (Lamentations 2:19)

Blessed is the one
   who does not walk in step with the wicked
or stand in the way that sinners take
   or sit in the company of mockers.
                       (Psalm 1:1)

The LORD is my light and my salvation—
   whom shall I fear?
The LORD is the stronghold of my life—
   of whom shall I be afraid?
                       (Psalm 27:1)

Have mercy on me, O God,
according to your unfailing love;
according to your great compassion
blot out my transgressions.

(Psalm 51:1)

But from everlasting to everlasting
the LORD's love is with those who fear him,
and his righteousness with their children's children—
with those who keep his covenant
and remember to obey his precepts.

(Psalm 103:17-18)

Unless the LORD builds the house,
the builders labor in vain.
Unless the LORD watches over the city,
the guards stand watch in vain.
In vain you rise early
and stay up late,
toiling for food to eat—
for he grants sleep to those he loves.
Children are a heritage from the LORD,
offspring a reward from him.
Like arrows in the hands of a warrior
are children born in one's youth.

(Psalm 127:1-4)

Listen, my son, to your father's instruction
and do not forsake your mother's teaching.
They are a garland to grace your head
and a chain to adorn your neck.

(Proverbs 1:8-9)

My son, do not forget my teaching,
but keep my commands in your heart,
for they will prolong your life many years
and bring you peace and prosperity.

(Proverbs 3:1-2)

The LORD's curse is on the house of the wicked,
but he blesses the home of the righteous.

(Proverbs 3:33)

Gracious words are a honeycomb,
  sweet to the soul and healing to the bones.
             (Proverbs 16:24)

Discipline your children, and they will give you peace;
  they will bring you the delights you desire.
             (Proverbs 29:17)

Start children off on the way they should go,
  and even when they are old they will not turn from it.
             (Proverbs 22:6)

The father of a righteous child has great joy;
  a man who fathers a wise son rejoices in him.
May your father and mother rejoice;
  may she who gave you birth be joyful!
             (Proverbs 23:24-25)

"I will contend with those who contend with you,
  and your children I will save."
             (Isaiah 49:25)

Children, obey your parents in the Lord, for this is right. "Honor your father and mother"—which is the first commandment with a promise— "so that it may go well with you and that you may enjoy long life on the earth" (Ephesians 6:1-3).

"If you, then, though you are evil, know how to give good gifts to your children, how much more will your Father in heaven give good gifts to those who ask him!" (Matthew 7:11).

"If you keep my commands, you will remain in my love, just as I have kept my Father's commands and remain in his love. I have told you this so that my joy may be in you and that your joy may be complete" (John 15:10-11).

Let us not become weary in doing good, for at the proper time we will reap a harvest if we do not give up (Galatians 6:9).

Do not be anxious about anything, but in every situation, by prayer and petition, with thanksgiving, present your requests to God. And the peace of God, which transcends all understanding, will guard your hearts and your minds in Christ Jesus (Philippians 4:6-7).

I have no greater joy than to hear that my children are walking in the truth (3 John 4).

The Happy Mom Discussion Guide

Introduction: Ditch the Crowd

Do you relate with feeling stressed out, pooped out, and over-whelmed much of the time as a mom? What needs to change in order for you to be more rested and content as a mom?

What do you hope to learn from reading this book?

What parenting concerns do you have right now?

Do you tend to be more of a "Tell me more" person or an "I already know that" person?

Key 1: Becoming Healthy

Are you sometimes like the Grumpy Mom who says, "It only goes downhill from there"? What's one thing you can do to break this negative pattern of thinking?

Talk about your priorities and how they play out in your everyday life. If you are married, can you tell your husband is higher than your children in the pecking order?

Environment trumps willpower when it comes to food. What is the nutritional environment of your home? How many times a week do you dine out (fast food or otherwise)? What's one thing you can do to eat healthier?

Describe the amount of exercise you get weekly.

Do you ever get the "cupcake spirit"? (To clarify, that's not when you eat cupcakes till you drop. It's when you commit to doing something unnecessary that will stress you out.) If so, give an example.

Do you get seven to eight hours of sleep every night? If not, what is preventing you from getting more sleep? What's one thing you could do this week to catch more z's?

Time for Vitamin G: Share five things you are thankful for about your children (review what you wrote down in "Today's Energy Boost" at the end of Day 5).

Share a time when you were fearful about something regarding your children. How did God see you through that time?

Key 2: Becoming Action-Oriented

When speaking to your children, how often do you raise your voice, yell, repeat yourself, threaten, promise, or beg ? What would be a more effective way to communicate?

If your third grader forgot his or her lunch, would you bring it to school? Why or why not?

If you have tweens or teens, talk about the hormonal and other changes you are seeing in your child.

What's one thing you can do to learn about the next stage of parenting you will enter?

Does your child regularly think, *Whoa, she really did mean it!* or the opposite?

In Day 11 we talked about the broken-window theory ("fix small things before they become bigger things"). What is one small thing in your child's behavior you want to notice and correct this week?

Also in Day 11 we talked about "Don't wait, create." What's one thing your child needs to practice at home this week? It could be greeting an adult properly, sitting through a meal without electronics to entertain, or practicing for a summer job interview.

Do you struggle with mommy guilt? What is the difference between bad guilt and good guilt?

Do you have understood screen time limits for your family? Are you happy with how and how long your children use screens? How about for yourself? If you need to make some changes, begin with making mealtime a screen-free zone for everyone.

How do you push "reset" or how would you like to push "reset" in the future? Weekly coffee date with a friend? Journaling? Prayer at the end of each day?

Key 3: Becoming Prayerful

When you have a problem, do you turn to your phone or computer to google an answer?

Read aloud the verses about wisdom found on pages 99-100 in Day 15.

What's one way you can become a more prayerful mom this week?

Have you ever participated in a Moms in Prayer group? Visit www.momsinprayer.org to see if there is a prayer group at the school your child attends. Consider beginning a prayer group with the moms you are doing this discussion with.

Share a time the Lord answered your prayers when a child was going haywire (see Day 17).

Spend time praying together now for your children. Here's a prayer guide to use if you'd like:

> *Praise:* Lord, I praise You that You will never leave us or forsake us.
>
> *Confession:* Lord, we silently confess our sins to You.
>
> *Thanksgiving:* Thank You for providing everything we need.
>
> *Intercession:* God, I pray that You will give _____ Your Spirit so he/she will not be timid, but have power and love and be self-disciplined (2 Timothy 1:7).

Key 4: Becoming Perseverant

Where's your favorite hideout from the kids? The laundry room? Bathroom? Starbucks? Social media?

When was the last time you did something to rejuvenate yourself as a mom? What did you do?

Say it out loud: *I am a mighty warrior mom* (see Day 20). Now talk about it in your group. Do you believe that to be true of you?

What Goliaths do you need to let your children face today instead of rescuing them?

Share a time your child has called you a "mean mom." Encourage one another in that. After all, motherhood is not a popularity contest and being a mean mom can be considered a great compliment.

What's something funny your child has done or said this week?

Who is a role model you can follow as a mother? This can be someone you know or someone you don't know personally.

"You're not raising children. You're raising adults." Do you agree with this? Are your children becoming less and less dependent on you? Do you allow reality to be a teacher, or do you solve problems for your child?

Key 5: Becoming Yes-Filled

What do you think about John Rosemond's Good Mommy Club (see Day 26)? Have you unwittingly subscribed to the doctrine of the Good Mommy Club?

Schedule an International Mommy-Take-a-Day-Off Day. Report how the day goes to the group. Or talk about it now if you've already enjoyed the holiday.

Do you struggle with the race to replicate? In what ways do you see yourself trying to keep up with the Joneses at some level?

How can you fit in more free play into your child's routine?

Do you have fun and laugh every single day? If not, how can you change that?

Is there a service project you do as a family? If not, what is something you might try in the future?

Share your chore success stories. What's working in your home?

Are you facing something that feels like mission impossible in your parenting right now? Describe what that is.

Use the year your youngest child will graduate from high school to project when you will have an empty nest. How does that date give you perspective or motivation today? What is your attitude about experiencing the empty nest?

Wrap-Up Questions

Which of the five keys in the acronym HAPPY challenged you the most?

> H: Becoming *Healthy*
> A: Becoming *Action-Oriented*
> P: Becoming *Prayerful*
> P: Becoming *Perseverant*
> Y: Becoming *Yes-Filled*

What changes have occurred in your attitude and mindset in the last thirty-one days?

Share a sweet moment that occurred between you and your child since you've read the book.

What was an aha moment for you while reading?

What is something you learned about being a happier mom?

What are a few specific things you will continue to do after this thirty-one-day experiment is over?

1.

2.

3.

Acknowledgments

A huge thank you to the happy moms who allowed me to interview them. I still marvel at the caliber of experts in the pages of this book. I'm very grateful for your input and influence.

Dr. Jennifer Degler—You've helped me and so many others fan the flame in our marriages. Meeting you last year was a huge highlight. Who knew car rides to the airport could be so much fun? I'm so glad to call you friend. James is glad too—go CWIVES!

Karen Ehman—Thank you for teaching me to *Keep It Shut* and *Let It Go*! You've been a wonderful friend and encourager since the first time I sat in your Hearts at Home session years ago. You are generous, tender, welcoming, and downright funny.

Pam Farrel—Easy to choose joy with a friend and mentor like you! Thank you for your shining example of how to raise sons who honor God and honor you. Can't say thank you enough for believing in me.

Dannah Gresh—Noelle and I attended our first Secret Keeper Girl event this year. Thank you for investing your life so girls can experience Pure Freedom. Your books are preparing me for the tween and teen years. I'm going to have some great dates with my kids because of you!

Hannah Keeley—From the first time we talked on the phone, I knew I had a kindred spirit in you, crazy mama who loves Jesus! I won't look at a DingDong the same way since I interviewed you. That is not food.

Karol Ladd—You are a dear example to me. I want to be a positive mom and positive author like you. What a joy to partner in ministry and be sisters in Christ. I will be throwing parties with a purpose and keeping a bowl of trail mix for my kids' friends with you in mind!

Kathi Lipp—You give the Bad Moms Club a good name. Your heart to help others is so beautiful. You help us write brave. Thank you for your glorious sense of humor that always makes me laugh.

Fern Nichols—Spending time with you is a precious gift. You are such a light for Jesus and your passion for prayer is infectious. My kids' lives and my life will be forever changed by the ministry of Moms in Prayer—thank you for that incredible blessing!

Laura Petherbridge—It was a divine appointment to meet at AWSA in Atlanta last summer. Your insights about being a smart stepmom add so much to the book. I love your practicality, enthusiasm, and heart for God.

Rhonda Rhea—You, my chocolate-loving friend, are an endless resource for good material! God zapped your family with fun genes. What a blessing to meet you and your girls last year. Your joy touches all around you for the better.

John Rosemond—Meeting you before my book deadline was a huge present from God. What a crack up to hear you say many things James tells me all the time, but you have the credentials to back it up! If every mom in America could hear you speak for just one hour, it would transform our culture in the best of ways.

Ruth Schwenk—Thank you for taking the time amidst your own book deadlines to talk about being a happy mom. I admire your intentionality in your family life. You're inspiring many to be better moms…thank you for leading the charge!

Kendra Smiley—How kind of you to have a last name to coordinate perfectly with my book. What a blessing your friendship has been. Your zany, fun personality plus John's even keel have produced some outstanding kids and grandkids. You are truly rich!

Gwen Smith—You introduced me to the modern marvels of dry shampoo and Keurig coffee. You taught me how to create better pins. This is what girlfriends do! I love you, dear Gwen. You are all in for Jesus; a woman who worships with her whole life.

Janet Thompson—Thank you for pouring yourself into mentoring other women. You can relate to the child who's lost a parent, to the woman who's been divorced, to the mom who's praying for a prodigal and so much more. Thanks for sharing your godly wisdom with us.

Kristen Welch—Reading your blog is always worthwhile. Thank you for sharing your story so we can teach our kids to serve more, love others, and whine less. Your *yes* is inspiring moms around the world to say *yes* to Jesus too.

To my Moms in Prayer Group—Thank you Liz, Elise, Beverly, and Marina for your faithfulness in prayer. Thank you for lifting up my kids to God's throne. And thank you, Clare, for partnering to pray for God's blessing on this book.

To my Harvest House family—Thank you so much for embracing my Happy Home series with open arms! We can accomplish much in thirty-one days. Thanks especially to my excellent editor, Rod Morris, and to LaRae Weikert, Bob Hawkins Jr., Christianne Debysingh, Brad Moses, and Shane White. A big shout out to Ben Laurro at Pure Publicity for getting me to New York City for every book so far (no pressure there, friend).

To my mother, Ann, and mother-in-love, Marilyn—Thank you for your generous love to me. Your words have encouraged me through the years. Thank you for being happy moms and (very) happy grandmas!

To my James—You sure do make it a lot easier to be a happy mom. Thank you for being the Alpha Dog around here. Long live the benevolent dictator! You put the happy in our home every day. Can't wait to go in-line skating again (wink wink). Acts of service, baby…

To my kids, Ethan, Noelle, and Lucy—A million thank yous for allowing me to put your stories in print. Now that you're getting older, there's a little more humiliation involved in your mom being an author and speaker. Riches in heaven (and maybe I'll take you out to ice cream here on earth?). I cannot express how blessed I am to be your mother. Thank you for making me a very happy (and proud) mom! I love you.

About Arlene Pellicane

Arlene and her happy husband, James, live in San Diego, California, with their three children, Ethan, Noelle, and Lucy. Arlene is also the author of *31 Days to Becoming a Happy Wife* and *31 Days to a Happy Husband*. She is the coauthor with Dr. Gary Chapman of *Growing Up Social: Raising Relational Kids in a Screen-Driven World*. Before becoming a stay-at-home mom, Arlene worked as the associate producer for *Turning Point Television with Dr. David Jeremiah* as well as a features producer for *The 700 Club*. She received her BA from Biola University and her master's in journalism from Regent University.

Arlene has appeared as a guest on the *Today Show, Fox & Friends, Focus on the Family, Family Life Today, The 700 Club,* and *Turning Point with Dr. David Jeremiah*. An energetic communicator, she shares humorous and compelling stories to guide women to positive life change. For free resources along with information about contacting Arlene to speak at your event, visit www.ArlenePellicane.com.

Visit Arlene's website for bonus material

www.ArlenePellicane.com

- Listen to Arlene's podcast for the interviews of many moms featured in this book, such as Dannah Gresh, Karen Ehman, and Kathi Lipp.
- Enhance your reading with corresponding videos from Arlene.
- Interact with Arlene through her blog.
- Sign up for Arlene's free monthly newsletter with tips for the happy home.

To learn more about Harvest House books
and to read sample chapters, visit our website:

www.harvesthousepublishers.com

HARVEST HOUSE PUBLISHERS
EUGENE, OREGON